PENGUIN BOOKS — GREAT IDEAS

Travels in the Land of Kubilai Khan

Marco Polo
1254–1324

Marco Polo

*Travels in the Land of
Kubilai Khan*

TRANSLATED BY
RONALD LATHAM

PENGUIN BOOKS — GREAT IDEAS

PENGUIN BOOKS

Published by the Penguin Group
Penguin Books Ltd, 80 Strand, London WC2R ORL, England
Penguin Group (USA) Inc., 375 Hudson Street, New York, New York 10014, USA
Penguin Group (Canada), 10 Alcorn Avenue, Toronto, Ontario, Canada M4V 3B2
(a division of Pearson Penguin Canada Inc.)
Penguin Ireland, 25 St Stephen's Green, Dublin 2, Ireland
(a division of Penguin Books Ltd)
Penguin Group (Australia), 250 Camberwell Road,
Camberwell, Victoria 3124, Australia (a division of Pearson Australia Group Pty Ltd)
Penguin Books India Pvt Ltd, 11 Community Centre,
Panchsheel Park, New Delhi – 110 017, India
Penguin Group (NZ), cnr Airborne and Rosedale Roads, Albany,
Auckland 1310, New Zealand (a division of Pearson New Zealand Ltd)
Penguin Books (South Africa) (Pty) Ltd, 24 Sturdee Avenue,
Rosebank 2196, South Africa

Penguin Books Ltd, Registered Offices: 80 Strand, London WC2R ORL, England

www.penguin.com

The Travels first published in Penguin Classics 1958
This extract published in Penguin Books 2005

1

Translation copyright © Ronald Latham, 1958

Taken from the Penguin Classics edition *The Travels*,
translated and edited by Ronald Latham

Set by Rowland Phototypesetting Ltd, Bury St Edmunds, Suffolk
Printed in England by Clays Ltd, St Ives plc

Contents

The Road to Cathay

You must know that after Chinghiz Khan the next ruler was Kuyuk Khan, the third Batu Khan, the fourth Altou Khan, the fifth Mongu Khan and the sixth Kubilai Khan, who is greater and more powerful than any of the others. For all the other five put together would not have such power as belongs to Kubilai. And here is a greater claim still, which I can confidently assert: that all the emperors of the world and all the kings of Christians and of Saracens combined would not possess such power or be able to accomplish so much as this same Kubilai, the Great Khan. And this I will clearly demonstrate to you in this book.

You should know that all the great lords who are of the lineage of Chinghiz Khan are conveyed for burial to a great mountain called Altai. When one of them dies, even if it be at a distance of a hundred days' journey from this mountain, he must be brought here for burial. And here is a remarkable fact: when the body of a Great Khan is being carried to this mountain – be it forty days' journey or more or less – all those who are encountered along the route by which the body is being conveyed are put to the sword by the attendants who are escorting it. 'Go!' they cry, 'and serve your lord in the next world.' For they truly believe that all those whom they put to death must go and serve the Khan in the next world.

And they do the same thing with horses: when the Khan dies, they kill all his best horses, so that he may have them in the next world. It is a fact that, when Mongu Khan died, more than 20,000 men were put to death, having encountered his body on the way to burial.

Since we have begun to speak of the Tartars, I have much to tell you about them. They spend the winter in steppes and warm regions where there is good grazing and pasturage for their beasts. In summer they live in cool regions, among mountains and valleys, where they find water and woodland as well as pasturage. A further advantage is that in cooler regions there are no horse-flies or gad-flies or similar pests to annoy them and their beasts. They spend two or three months climbing steadily and grazing as they go, because if they confined their grazing to one spot there would not be grass enough for the multitude of their flocks.

They have circular houses made of wood and covered with felt, which they carry about with them on four-wheeled wagons wherever they go. For the framework of rods is so neatly and skilfully constructed that it is light to carry. And every time they unfold their house and set it up, the door is always facing south. They also have excellent two-wheeled carts covered with black felt, of such good design that if it rained all the time the rain would never wet anything in the cart. These are drawn by oxen and camels. And in these carts they carry their wives and children and all they need in the way of utensils.

And I assure you that the womenfolk buy and sell and do all that is needful for their husbands and households. For the men do not bother themselves about anything but hunting and warfare and falconry. They live on meat and milk and game and on Pharaoh's rats, which are abundant everywhere in the steppes. They have no objection to eating the flesh of horses and dogs and drinking mares' milk. In fact they eat flesh of any sort. Not for anything in the world would one of them touch another's wife; they are too well assured that such a deed is wrongful and disgraceful. The wives are true and loyal to their husbands and very good at their household tasks. Even if there are as many as ten or twenty of them in one household, they live together in a concord and unity beyond praise, so that you would never hear a harsh word spoken. They all devote themselves to their various tasks and the care of the children, who are held among them in common. Their mode of marriage is such that any man may take as many wives as he pleases, even up to a hundred, if he is able to support them. The husband gives a dowry to his wife's mother; the wife gives nothing to the husband. You must understand that the first wife is reckoned the best and enjoys the highest status. Because they have so many wives, they have more children than other men. They may marry their cousins; and, when a father dies, the eldest son marries his father's wives, excluding his own mother. He may also marry his brother's wife, if the brother dies. When they take a wife, they hold a great wedding celebration.

I will now tell you of their religion. They say that there is a High God, exalted and heavenly, to whom they offer daily prayer with thurible and incense, but only for a sound understanding and good health. They also have a god of their own whom they call Natigai.

They say that he is an earthly god and watches over their children, their beasts, and their crops. They pay him great reverence and honour; for each man has one in his house. They make this god of felt and cloth and keep him in their house; and they also make the god's wife and children. They set his wife at his left hand and his children in front. And they treat them with great reverence. When they are about to have a meal, they take a lump of fat and smear the god's mouth with it, and the mouths of his wife and children. Then they take some broth and pour it outside the door of the house. When they have done this, they say that their god and his household have had their share. After this they eat and drink. You should know that they drink mare's milk; but they subject it to a process that makes it like white wine and very good to drink, and they call it *koumiss*.

As to their costume, the rich wear cloth of gold and silk and rich furs – sable and ermine and miniver and fox. And all their trappings are very fine and very costly. Their weapons are bows and swords and clubs; but they rely mainly on their bows, for they are excellent archers. On their backs they wear an armour of buffalo hide or some other leather which is very tough.

They are stout fighters, excelling in courage and hardihood. Let me explain how it is that they can endure more than any other men. Often enough, if need be, they will go or stay for a whole month without provisions, drinking only the milk of a mare and eating wild game of their own taking. Their horses, meanwhile, support themselves by grazing, so that there is no need to carry barley or straw. They are very obedient to their masters.

In case of need they will stay all night on horseback under arms, while their mount goes on steadily cropping the grass. They are of all men in the world the best able to endure exertion and hardship and the least costly to maintain and therefore the best adapted for conquering territory and overthrowing kingdoms.

Now the plan on which their armies are marshalled is this. When a lord of the Tartars goes out to war with a following of 100,000 horsemen, he has them organized as follows. He has one captain in command of every ten, one of every hundred, one of every thousand and one of every ten-thousand, so that he never needs to consult with more than ten men. In the same way each commander of ten-thousand or a thousand or a hundred consults only with his ten immediate subordinates, and each man is answerable to his own chief. When the supreme commander wishes to send someone on some operation, he orders the commander of ten-thousand to give him a thousand men; the latter orders the captain of a thousand to contribute his share. So the order is passed down, each commander being required to furnish his quota towards the thousand. At each stage it is promptly received and executed. For they are all obedient to the word of command more than any other people in the world. You should know that the unit of 100,000 is called a *tuk*, that of 10,000 a *tomaun*, and there are corresponding terms for the thousands, the hundreds, and the tens.

When an army sets out on some operation, whether it be in the plains or in the mountains, 200 men are sent two days' ride in advance as scouts, and as many to the rear and on the flanks; that is four scouting parties in all. And this they do so that the army cannot be attacked without warning.

When they are going on a long expedition, they carry no baggage with them. They each carry two leather flasks to hold the milk they drink and a small pot for cooking meat. They also carry a small tent to shelter them from the rain. In case of need, they will ride a good ten days' journey without provisions and without making a fire, living only on the blood of their horses; for every rider pierces a vein of his horse and drinks the blood. They also have their dried milk, which is solid like paste; and this is how they dry it. First they bring the milk to the boil. At the appropriate moment they skim off the cream that floats on the surface and put it in another vessel to be made into butter, because so long as it remained the milk could not be dried. Then they stand the milk in the sun and leave it to dry. When they are going on an expedition, they take about ten pounds of this milk; and every morning they take out about half a pound of it and put it in a small leather flask, shaped like a gourd, with as much water as they please. Then, while they ride, the milk in the flask dissolves into a fluid, which they drink. And this is their breakfast.

When they join battle with their enemies, these are the tactics by which they prevail. They are never ashamed to have recourse to flight. They manoeuvre freely, shooting at the enemy, now from this quarter, now from that. They have trained their horses so well that they wheel this way or that as quickly as a dog would do. When they are pursued and take to flight, they fight as well and as effectively as when they are face to face with the enemy. When they are fleeing at top speed, they twist round with their bows and let fly their arrows to such good purpose that they kill the horses of the enemy and the riders too. When the enemy thinks he has routed and crushed them, then he is lost; for he finds his horses killed and not a few of his men. As soon as the Tartars decide that they have killed enough of the pursuing horses and horsemen, they wheel round and attack and acquit themselves so well and so courageously that they gain a complete victory. By these tactics they have already won many battles and conquered many nations.

All that I have told you concerns the usages and customs of the genuine Tartars. But nowadays their stock has degenerated. Those who live in Cathay have adopted the manners and customs of the idolaters and abandoned their own faith, while those who live in the Levant have adopted the manners of the Saracens.

Let me tell you next of the Tartar fashion of maintaining justice. For a petty theft, not amounting to a capital offence, the culprit receives seven strokes of the rod, or seventeen or twenty-seven or thirty-seven or forty-seven, ascending thus by tens to 107 in proportion to the magnitude of his crime. And many die of this flogging. If the offender has stolen a horse or otherwise incurred the death penalty, he is chopped in two by the sword. If, however, he can afford to pay, and is prepared to pay nine times the value of what he has stolen, he escapes other punishment.

All the great lords, and other owners of flocks and herds, including horses, mares, camels, oxen, cows, and other large beasts, have them branded with their own mark. Then they turn them loose to graze on the plains and hillsides with no herdsman to guard them. If the herds intermingle, each beast is duly returned to the owner whose mark it bears. Their sheep and rams are entrusted to the care of shepherds. All their beasts are of great size and fat and exceedingly fine.

Here is another strange custom which I had forgotten to describe. You may take it for a fact that, when there are two men of whom one has had a male child who has died at the age of four, or what you will, and the other has had a female child who has also died, they arrange a marriage between them. They give the dead girl to the dead boy as a wife and draw up a deed of matrimony. Then they burn this deed, and declare that the smoke that rises into the air goes to their children in the other world and that they get wind of it and regard themselves as husband and wife. They hold a great wedding feast and scatter some of the food here and there and declare that that too goes to their children in the other world. And here is something else that they do. They draw pictures on paper of men in the guise of slaves, and of horses, clothes, coins, and furniture and then burn them; and they declare that all these become the possessions of their children in the next world. When they have done this, they consider themselves to be kinsfolk and uphold their kinship just as firmly as if the children were alive.

Now I have given you an unvarnished account of the usages and customs of the Tartars. Not that I have told you of the lofty state of the Great Khan, the Great Lord of all the Tartars, or of his high imperial court. I will tell you all about them in this book in due time and place. For they are truly wonderful things to set down in writing. Meanwhile, let us resume the thread of our discourse in the great plain where we were when we began to talk about the doings of the Tartars.

If the traveller leaves Karakorum and Altai, where, as I have told you, the Tartars bury their dead, and journeys towards the north, he traverses a country called the plain of Bargu, which extends for forty days' journey. The inhabitants, who are called Mekrit, are a savage race. Their livelihood depends on beasts, mostly reindeer, which they even use for riding. They resemble the Tartars in their customs and are subject to the Great Khan. They have neither corn nor wine. In summer they have plenty of game for hunting, both beasts and birds; but in winter neither beast nor bird lives there because of the great cold. The birds especially congregate during the moulting season in summer round the numerous lakes, meres, and marshes; and when they have shed all their old plumage, so that they cannot fly, the hunters take as many as they want. They also live on fish.

At the end of forty days, the traveller reaches the Ocean. Here there are mountains where peregrine falcons build their nests. You must understand that there are neither men nor women here, nor beasts nor birds, except a species of bird called *bargherlac* on which the falcons prey. They are of the size of partridges and have feet like parrots and tails like swallows. They are strong fliers. When the Great Khan wants eyasses of the peregrine falcon, he sends for them all the way to this district.

The islands in this ocean breed gerfalcons. I assure you that this region is so far north that the Pole Star is left behind towards the south. The gerfalcons of which I have spoken are so abundant here that the Great Khan has as many of them as he wants. So you must not suppose that those who export them from Christendom to the Tartars send them to the Great Khan; they actually export them to the Khan of the Levant, to Arghun or whoever it may be.

[. . .]

If we leave this province and city and go on our way for three days, we shall find a city called Chagan-nor where there is a large palace belonging to the Great Khan. He enjoys staying in this palace because there are lakes and rivers here in plenty, well stocked with swans. There are also fine plains, teeming with cranes, pheasants and partridges, and many other sorts of wild fowl; and that is a further attraction for the Great Khan, who is a keen sportsman and takes great delight in hawking for birds with falcons and gerfalcons. There are five sorts of crane, which I will describe to you. One is entirely black, like a raven, and very large. The second is pure white. Its wings are beautiful, with all the plumage studded with round eyes like those of a peacock but of the colour of burnished gold. It has a scarlet and black head and a black and white neck and is larger than any of the others. The third species is like the cranes we know. The fourth is small, with long plumes by its ears, scarlet and black in colour and very beautiful. The fifth is a very large bird, quite grey with shapely head coloured scarlet and black.

Beyond this city lies a valley in which the Great Khan keeps flocks of *cators*, which we call 'great partridges', in such quantities that they are a sight to behold. In order to feed them, he regularly has crops sown on the slopes in summer, consisting of millet and panic and other favourite foods of such fowl, and allows no one to reap them, so that they may eat their fill. And many guards are set to watch these birds, to prevent anyone from taking them. And in winter their keepers scatter millet for them; and they are so used to this feeding that, if a man flings some of the grain on the ground, he has only to whistle and, wherever they may be, they flock to him. And the Great Khan has had many huts built, in which they spend the night. So, when he visits this country, he has a plentiful supply of these fowl, as many as he wants. And in winter, when they are nice and plump, since he does not stay there himself at this season because of the intense cold, he has camel-loads of them brought to him, wherever he may be.

When the traveller leaves this city and journeys north-north-east for three days, he comes to a city called Shang-tu, which was built by the Great Khan now reigning, whose name is Kubilai. In this city Kubilai Khan built a huge palace of marble and other ornamental stones. Its halls and chambers are all gilded, and the whole building is marvellously embellished and richly adorned. At one end it extends into the middle of the city; at the other it abuts on the city wall. At this end another wall, running out from the city wall in the direction opposite to the palace, encloses and encircles fully sixteen miles of park-land well watered with springs and streams and diversified with lawns. Into this park there is no entry except by way of the palace. Here the Great Khan keeps game animals of all sorts, such as hart, stag, and roebuck, to provide food for the gerfalcons and other falcons which he has here in mew. The gerfalcons alone amount to more than 200. Once a week he comes in person to inspect them in the mew. Often, too, he enters the park with a leopard on the crupper of his horse; when he feels inclined, he lets it go and thus catches a hart or stag or roebuck to give to the gerfalcons that he keeps in mew. And this he does for recreation and sport.

In the midst of this enclosed park, where there is a beautiful grove, the Great Khan has built another large palace, constructed entirely of canes, but with the interior all gilt and decorated with beasts and birds of very skilful workmanship. It is reared on gilt and varnished pillars, on each of which stands a dragon, entwining the pillar with his tail and supporting the roof on his outstretched limbs. The roof is also made of canes, so well varnished that it is quite waterproof. Let me explain how it is constructed. You must know that these canes are more than three palms in girth and from ten to fifteen paces long. They are sliced down through the middle from one knot to the next, thus making two shingles. These shingles are thick and long enough not only for roofing but for every sort of construction. The palace, then, is built entirely of such canes. As a protection against the wind each shingle is fastened with nails. And the Great Khan has had it so designed that it can be moved whenever he fancies; for it is held in place by more than 200 cords of silk.

The Great Khan stays at Shang-tu for three months in the year, June, July, and August, to escape from the heat and for the sake of the recreation it affords. During these three months he keeps the palace of canes erected; for the rest of the year it is dismantled. And he has had it so constructed that he can erect or dismantle it at pleasure.

When it comes to the 28th day of August, the Great Khan takes his leave of this city and of this palace. Every year he leaves on this precise day; and I will tell you why. The fact is that he has a stud of snow-white stallions and snow-white mares, without a speck of any other colour. Their numbers are such that the mares alone amount to more than 10,000. The milk of these mares may not be drunk by anyone who is not of the imperial lineage, that is to say of the lineage of the Great Khan. To this rule there is one exception; the milk may be drunk by a race of men called Horiat, by virtue of a special privilege granted to them by Chinghiz Khan because of a victory that they won with him in the old days. When these white steeds are grazing, such reverence is shown to them that if a great lord were going that way he could not pass through their midst, but would either wait till they had passed or go on until he had passed them. The astrologers and idolaters have told the Great Khan that he must make a libation of the milk of these mares every year on the 28th August, flinging it into the air and on the earth, so that the spirits may have their share to drink. They must have this, it is said, in order that they may guard all his possessions, men and women, beasts, birds, crops, and everything besides.

For this purpose the Great Khan leaves this palace and goes elsewhere. But, before we follow him, let me tell you of a strange thing which I had forgotten. You must know that, when the Great Khan was staying in his palace and the weather was rainy or cloudy, he had wise astrologers and enchanters who by their skill and their enchantments would dispel all the clouds and the bad weather from above the palace so that, while bad weather continued all around, the weather above the palace was fine. The wise men who do this are called Tibetans and Kashmiris; these are two races of men who practise idolatry. They know more of diabolic arts and enchantments than any other men. They do what they do by the arts of the Devil; but they make others believe that they do it by great holiness and by the work of God. For this reason they go about filthy and begrimed, with no regard for their own decency or for the persons who behold them; they keep the dirt on their faces, never wash or comb, but always remain in a state of squalor. These men have a peculiar custom, of which I will tell you. When a man is condemned to die and is put to death by the authorities, they take the body and cook and eat it. But, if anyone dies a natural death, they would never think of eating him.

Here is another remarkable fact about these enchanters, or *Bakhshi** as they are called. I assure you that,

---

* A special religious order, like the Dominican or Franciscan Friars.

when the Great Khan is seated in his high hall at his table, which is raised more than eight cubits above the floor, and the cups are on the floor of the hall, a good ten paces distant from the table, and are full of wine and milk and other pleasant drinks, these *Bakhshi* contrive by their enchantment and their art that the full cups rise up of their own accord from the floor on which they have been standing and come to the Great Khan without anyone touching them. And this they do in the sight of 10,000 men. What I have told you is the plain truth without a word of falsehood. And those who are skilled in necromancy will confirm that it is perfectly feasible.

Here is a further fact about these *Bakhshi*. When the feast-days of their idols come round, they go to the Great Khan and say: 'Sire, the feast of such-and-such of our idols is approaching.' And they mention the name of some idol, whichever they may choose, and then continue: 'You are aware, Sire, that it is the practice of this idol to cause bad weather and damage to our property and to cattle and crops unless it receives oblations and holocausts. We accordingly beseech you, Sire, that we may be given so many black-faced sheep, so much incense, so much aloes wood, so much of this and so much of that, so that we may offer great worship and sacrifice to our idols in order that they may save us, our bodies, cattle, and crops.' This they say to the barons who surround the Great Khan and to those who hold authority under him. And these repeat their words to the Great Khan, so that the *Bakhshi* have everything they ask for in order to celebrate the feast of their idol. Thereupon they proceed to perform their rites with much chanting and festivity. For they regale their idols with fragrant incense from these sweet spices; and they cook the meat and set it before them and sprinkle some of the gravy here and there, declaring that the idols are taking as much of it as they want. That is how they do honour to their idols on their feast-days.

You may take it for a fact that all the idols have their own feasts on the days assigned to them, just as our saints have. They have huge monasteries and abbeys, of such a size that I assure you that some resemble small cities inhabited by more than 2,000 monks according to their usage, who are better dressed than other men. They wear their heads and chins clean-shaven. They make the most magnificent feasts for their idols with the most magnificent hymns and illuminations that were ever seen.

A further point about these *Bakhshi* is that among their other privileges they are entitled according to their order to take wives. And so they do, and rear children in plenty.

Besides these there is another order of devotees who are called *Sien-seng*. They are men of extreme abstinence according to their own observances, and lead a life of great austerity which I will describe to you. The plain truth is that all their lives long they eat nothing but bran, that is to say the husk left over from wheat flour. For they take wheaten grain and put it in hot water and leave it there a little while till all the kernel or marrow is separated from the husk; then they eat the bran that has been washed in this way, without anything to give it a flavour. They fast many times in the year, besides eating absolutely nothing but this bran of which I have told you. They have huge idols, and many of them, and sometimes they worship fire. The other devotees declare that those who live this life of abstinence are heretics, as it were Patarins, because they do not worship their idols in the same manner as the rest. There is one great difference between the two orders of devotees; those who observe the stricter rule would not take a wife for anything in the world. They also have their heads and chins shaven. They wear black and blue robes of sackcloth; if they should happen to wear silk, it is still of the same colours. They sleep on mats of wicker-work. Altogether they lead the most austere lives of any men in the world.

Their idols are all female, that is to say they all bear the names of women.

So much, then, for that. I will now tell you the truly amazing facts about the greatest lord of the Lords of all the Tartars, the right noble Great Khan whose name is Kubilai.

Kubilai Khan

I have come to the point in our book at which I will tell you of the great achievements of the Great Khan now reigning. The title Khan means in our language 'Great Lord of Lords'. And certainly he has every right to this title; for everyone should know that this Great Khan is the mightiest man, whether in respect of subjects or of territory or of treasure, who is in the world today or who ever has been, from Adam our first parent down to the present moment. And I will make it quite clear to you in our book that this is the plain truth, so that everyone will be convinced that he is indeed the greatest lord the world has ever known. Here, then, is my proof.

First, you should know that he is undoubtedly descended in the direct imperial line from Chinghiz Khan; for only one of that lineage may be Lord of all the Tartars. He is sixth in succession of the Great Khans of all the Tartars, having received the lordship and begun his reign in the year of Christ's nativity 1256. He won the lordship by his own valour and prowess and good sense; his kinsfolk and brothers tried to debar him from it, but by his great prowess he won it. And you must know that it was properly his by right. From the beginning of his reign down to the present year 1298 is a period of forty-two years. His age today may well be as much as eighty-five years. Before he became Khan, he used to go out regularly on military expeditions and he showed himself a valiant soldier and a good commander. But thereafter he went out only once; that was in 1286, and I will tell you how it came about.

The fact is that a certain man named Nayan, who was Kubilai's uncle, found himself while still a youth the lord and ruler of many lands and provinces, so that he could easily raise a force of 400,000 horsemen. Like his ancestors before him, he was subject to the Great Khan. But, seeing that he was a young man of thirty with so many men at his command, he resolved that he would be subject no longer but to the best of his ability would despoil his overlord of the suzerainty. This Nayan, then, sent envoys to Kaidu, who was a great and powerful lord and nephew to the Great Khan, but had rebelled against him and was his bitter enemy. He proposed that Kaidu should attack the Great Khan from one quarter while he himself advanced against him from the opposite one, so as to despoil him of land and lordship. Kaidu welcomed the proposal and promised to have his forces fully arrayed by the date fixed and to march against the Great Khan. And this he was well able to do; for he could put 100,000 horsemen in the field. What need of more words? These two barons, Nayan and Kaidu, made their preparations and mustered a great array of horse and foot to attack the Great Khan.

When the Great Khan got word of this plot, he was not unduly perturbed; but like a wise man of approved valour he began to marshal his own forces, declaring that he would never wear his crown or hold his land if he did not bring these two false traitors to an evil end.

He completed his preparations in twenty-two days, so secretly that no one knew anything about them except those of his own Council. He had assembled 260,000 cavalry and 100,000 infantry. The reason why he confined himself to this number was that these were drawn from the troops in his own immediate neighbourhood. His other armies, which were twelve in all and totalled an immense number of men, were so far away on campaigns of conquest in many parts that he could not have got them together at the right time and place. If he had assembled all his forces, he would have had as many horsemen as he could possibly desire and their numbers would have been past all reckoning or belief. The 360,000 men whom he actually levied were his falconers and other members of his personal bodyguard.

If he had summoned the armies which he keeps continually on guard over the provinces of Cathay, this would inevitably have consumed thirty or forty days. Moreover, the levy would have become common knowledge and Kaidu and Nayan would have joined forces and occupied strong and advantageous positions. But Kubilai intended by means of speed, the companion of victory, to forestall Nayan's preparations and catch him alone, because he could more easily defeat him alone than in conjunction with his ally.

This is a convenient place to record a few facts about the armies of the Great Khan. You should know that in all the provinces of Cathay and Manzi and in all the rest of his dominions there are many disaffected and disloyal subjects who, if they had the chance, would rebel against their lord. Accordingly, in every province where there are big cities and a large population he is obliged to maintain armies. These are stationed in the open country four or five miles from the cities, which are not allowed to have gates or walls so as to bar the ingress of anyone who chooses to enter. These armies the Great Khan changes every two years, and so likewise the captains who command them. And with this bridle to restrain them the people stay quiet, and cannot cause any disturbance or insurrection. Besides the pay which the Great Khan gives them regularly from the revenues of the provinces, these armies live on the immense herds of cattle that are assigned to them and on the milk which they send into the towns to sell in return for necessary provisions. They are stationed at various points, thirty, forty, or sixty days' journey apart.

When the Great Khan had mustered the mere handful of men of which I have spoken, he consulted his astrologers to learn whether he would defeat his enemies and bring his affairs to a happy issue. They assured him that he would deal with his enemies as he pleased. Thereupon he set out with all his forces and went on until after twenty days they came to a great plain where Nayan lay with all his forces, who were not less than 400,000 horsemen. They arrived early in the morning and caught the enemy completely unawares; the Great Khan had had all the roads so carefully watched that no one could come or go without being intercepted, and had thus ensured that the enemy had no suspicion of their approach. Indeed, when they arrived Nayan was in his tent, dallying in bed with his wife, to whom he was greatly attached.

What more shall I say? When the day of battle dawned, the Great Khan suddenly appeared on a mound that rose from the plain where Nayan's forces were bivouacked. They were quite at their ease, like men who had not the faintest suspicion that anyone was approaching with hostile intent. Indeed they felt so secure that they had posted no sentries round their camp and sent out no patrols to van or rear. And suddenly there was the Great Khan on the hill I have mentioned. He stood on the top of a wooden tower, full of crossbowmen and archers, which was carried by four elephants wearing stout leather armour draped with cloths of silk and gold. Above his head flew his banner with the emblem of the sun and moon, so high that it could be clearly seen on every side. His troops were marshalled in thirty squadrons of 10,000 mounted archers each, grouped in three divisions; and those on the left and right he flung out so that they encircled Nayan's camp in a moment. In front of every squadron of horse were 500 foot-soldiers with short pikes and swords. They were so trained that, whenever the cavalry purposed a retreat, they would jump on the horses' cruppers and flee with them; then, when the retreat was halted, they would dismount and slaughter the enemies' horses with their pikes. Such, then, was the formation in which the Great Khan's forces were drawn up round Nayan's camp in readiness for the battle.

When Nayan and his men saw the troops of the Great Khan surrounding their camp, they were utterly taken aback. They rushed to arms, arrayed themselves in haste, and formed their ranks in due order.

When both parties were lined up in battle array, so

that nothing remained but to come to blows, then might be heard a tumult of many instruments, the shrilling of fifes and sound of men singing at the pitch of their voices. For the usage of the Tartars is such that when they are confronting the foe and marshalled for the fray they do not join battle till the drums begin to beat – that is the drums of the commander. While they wait for the beat of the drums, all the Tartar host sound their instruments and join in song. That is why the noise of instruments and of singing was so loud on both sides alike.

When all the troops were in readiness on both sides, then the drums of the Great Khan began to beat. After that there was no more delay; but the two armies fell upon each other with bow and sword and club, and a few with lances. The foot-soldiers had cross-bows also and other weapons in plenty. What more shall I say? This was the start of a bitter and bloody battle. Now you might see arrows flying like pelting rain, for the whole air was full of them. Now you might see horsemen and horses tumbling dead upon the ground. So loud was the shouting and the clash of armies that you could not have heard the thunder of heaven. You must know that Nayan was a baptized Christian and in this battle he had the cross of Christ on his standard.

What need to make a long story of it? Enough that this was the most hazardous fight and the most fiercely contested that ever was seen. Never in our time were so many men engaged on one battlefield, especially so many horsemen. So many died on either side that it was a marvel to behold. The battle raged from daybreak till noon, and for a long time its issue hung in the balance;

Nayan's followers were so devoted to him, for he was an open-handed master, that they were ready to die rather than turn their backs. But in the end the victory fell to the Great Khan. When Nayan and his men saw that they could hold out no longer, they took to flight. But this availed them nothing; for Nayan was taken prisoner, and all his barons and his men surrendered to the Great Khan.

When the Great Khan learnt that Nayan was a prisoner, he commanded that he should be put to death. And this was how it was done. He was wrapped up tightly in a carpet and then dragged about so violently, this way and that, that he died. Their object in choosing this mode of death was so that the blood of the imperial lineage might not be spilt upon the earth, and that sun and air might not witness it.

After this victory all Nayan's men and barons did homage to the Great Khan and swore fealty to him. They were men of four different provinces named Chorcha, Kauli, Barskol, and Sikintinju.

After the Great Khan had won this victory, the various races of men who were there – Saracens, idolaters, and Jews, and many others who do not believe in God – made mock of the cross which Nayan had borne on his banner. They jeered at the Christians who were there: 'See how the cross of your God has helped Nayan, who was a Christian!' So unrestrained was their mockery and their jeering that it came to the ears of the Great Khan. Thereupon he rebuked those who mocked at the cross in his presence. Then he summoned many Christians who were there and began to comfort them. 'If the cross of your God has not helped Nayan,' he said, 'it was for a very good reason. Because it is good, it ought not to lend its aid except in a good and righteous cause. Nayan was a traitor who broke faith with his liege lord. Hence the fate that has befallen him was a vindication of the right. And the cross of your God did well in not helping against the right.' The Christians answered: 'Most mighty lord, what you say is quite true. The cross would not lend itself to wrong-doing and disloyalty like that of Nayan, who was a traitor to his liege lord. He has received what he well deserved.' Such were the words that passed between the Great Khan and the Christians about the cross that Nayan had borne on his standard.

After this victory over Nayan, the Great Khan returned to his capital of Khan-balik. And there he stayed, amid great rejoicing and merry-making.

As for that other rebellious baron, the prince whose name was Kaidu, when he heard of Nayan's defeat and death he was greatly perturbed and abandoned his campaign, for fear lest he might meet the same fate.

It was in the month of November that Kubilai returned to Khan-balik. And there he stayed till February and March, the season of our Easter. Learning that this was one of our principal feasts, he sent for all the Christians and desired them to bring him the book containing the four Gospels. After treating the book to repeated applications of incense with great ceremony, he kissed it devoutly and desired all his barons and lords there present to do the same. This usage he regularly observes on the principal feasts of the Christians, such as Easter and

Christmas. And he does likewise on the principal feasts of the Saracens, Jews, and idolaters. Being asked why he did so, he replied: 'There are four prophets who are worshipped and to whom all the world does reverence. The Christians say that their God was Jesus Christ, the Saracens Mahomet, the Jews Moses, and the idolaters Sakyamuni Burkhan, who was the first to be represented as God in the form of an idol. And I do honour and reverence to all four, so that I may be sure of doing it to him who is greatest in heaven and truest; and to him I pray for aid.' But on the Great Khan's own showing he regards as truest and best the faith of the Christians, because he declares that it commands nothing that is not full of all goodness and holiness. He will not on any account allow the Christians to carry the cross before them, and this because on it suffered and died such a great man as Christ.

Someone may well ask why, since he regards the Christian faith as the best, he does not embrace it and become a Christian. The reason may be gathered from what he said to Messer Niccolò and Messer Maffeo when he sent them as emissaries to the Pope. They used from time to time to raise this matter with him; but he would reply: 'On what grounds do you desire me to become a Christian? You see that the Christians who live in these parts are so ignorant that they accomplish nothing and are powerless. And you see that these idolaters do whatever they will; and when I sit at table the cups in the middle of the hall come to me full of wine or other beverages without anyone touching them, and I drink from them. They banish bad weather in any direction they choose and perform many marvels. And, as you know, their idols speak and give them such predictions as they ask. But, if I am converted to the faith of Christ and become a Christian, then my barons and others who do not embrace the faith of Christ will say to me: "What has induced you to undergo baptism and adopt the faith of Christ? What virtues or what miracles have you seen to his credit?" For these idolaters declare that what they do they do by their holiness and by virtue of their idols. Then I should not know what to answer, which would be a grave error in their eyes. And these idolaters, who by their arts and sciences achieve such great results, could easily compass my death. But do you go to your Pope and ask him on my behalf to send me a hundred men learned in your religion, who in the face of these idolaters will have the knowledge to condemn their performances and tell them that they too can do such things but will not, because they are done by diabolic art and evil spirits, and will show their mastery by making the idolaters powerless to perform these marvels in their presence. On the day when we see this, I too will condemn them and their religion. Then I will be baptized, and all my barons and magnates will do like-wise, and their subjects in turn will undergo baptism. So there will be more Christians here than there are in your part of the world.' And if, as was said at the beginning, men had really been sent by the Pope with the ability to preach our faith to the Great Khan, then assuredly he would have become a Christian. For it is known for a fact that he was most desirous to be converted.

★

You have heard how on this one campaign Kubilai led his army out to battle. On all his other enterprises or campaigns he used to send his sons or barons; but on this occasion he would have no one in command but himself, so serious and so culpable did he consider the rebellion of this baron. Let us now leave this subject and return to a recital of the great achievements of the Great Khan.

We have told you of his lineage and his age. We shall now relate how he dealt with those barons who acquitted themselves well in the battle and how with those who showed themselves cowards and poltroons. Of the former, he promoted those who were commanders of 100 men to the command of 1,000, and commanders of 1,000 to the command of 10,000; and he gave them lavish gifts of silver plate and tablets of authority, each according to his rank. For a commander of 100 has a tablet of silver; a commander of 1,000 a tablet of gold, or rather of silver gilt; and a commander of 10,000 a tablet of gold with a lion's head. The tablets of command over 100 or 1,000 weigh 120 *saggi* apiece, those with a lion's head weigh 220. On all these tablets is written a command in these words: 'By the might of the Great God and the great grace he has given to our Emperor, blessed be the name of the Khan, and death and destruction to all who do not obey him.' Let me add that all who have these tablets also have warrants setting forth in writing all the powers vested in them by their office.

As for the commander of 100,000, or the generalissimo of a great army, he has a tablet of gold weighing 300 *saggi*, with an inscription such as I have mentioned; and at the foot of the tablet is portrayed the lion, and above it is an image of the sun and moon. In addition he has warrants of high command and great authority. And whenever he goes riding he must carry an umbrella over his head in token of his exalted rank; and when he sits he must sit on a silver chair. To these dignitaries the Great Khan also gives a tablet with the sign of the gerfalcon; these tablets are given to the very great barons so that they may exercise full powers equivalent to his own. When one of them wishes to send a courier or other emissary, he is authorized to requisition a king's horses if he wishes; and when I say a king's horses, this naturally implies the horses of any other man.

Let me tell you next of the personal appearance of the Great Lord of Lords whose name is Kubilai Khan. He is a man of good stature, neither short nor tall but of moderate height. His limbs are well fleshed out and modelled in due proportion. His complexion is fair and ruddy like a rose, the eyes black and handsome, the nose shapely and set squarely in place.

He has four consorts who are all accounted his lawful wives; and his eldest son by any of these four has a rightful claim to be emperor on the death of the present Khan. They are called empresses, each by her own name. Each of these ladies holds her own court. None of them has less than 300 ladies in waiting, all of great beauty and charm. They have many eunuchs and many other men and women in attendance, so that each one of these ladies has in her court 10,000 persons. When he wishes to lie with one of his four wives, he invites her to his chamber; or sometimes he goes to his wife's chamber.

He also has many concubines, about whom I will tell you. There is a province inhabited by Tartars who are called Kungurat, which is also the name of their city. They are a very good-looking race with fair complexions. Every two years or so, according to his pleasure, the Great Khan sends emissaries to this province to select for him out of the most beautiful maidens, according to the standard of beauty which he lays down for them, some four or five hundred, more or less as he may decide. This is how the selection is made. When the emissaries arrive, they summon to their presence all the maidens of the province. And there valuers are deputed for the task. After inspecting and surveying every girl feature by feature, her hair, her face, her eyebrows, her mouth, her lips, and every other feature, to see whether they are well-formed and in harmony with her person, the valuers award to some a score of sixteen marks, to others seventeen, eighteen, or twenty, or more or less according to the degree of their beauty. And, if the Great Khan has ordered them to bring him all who score twenty marks, or perhaps twenty-one, according to the number ordered, these are duly brought. When they have come to his presence, he has them assessed a second time by other valuers, and then the thirty or forty with the highest score are selected for his chamber. These are first allotted, one by one, to the barons' wives, who are instructed to observe them carefully at night in their chambers, to make sure that they are virgins and not blemished or defective in any member, that they sleep sweetly without snoring, and that their breath is sweet and they give out no unpleasant odour. Then those who

30

are approved are divided into groups of six, who serve
the Khan for three days and three nights at a time in his
chamber and his bed, ministering to all his needs. And
he uses them according to his pleasure. After three days
and nights, in come the next six damsels. And so they
continue in rotation throughout the year. While some
of the group are in attendance in their lord's chamber,
the others are waiting in an ante-chamber hard by. If he
is in need of anything from outside, such as food or
drink, the damsels inside the chamber pass word to those
outside, who immediately get it ready. In this way the
Khan is served by no one except these damsels. As for
the other damsels, who are rated at a lower score, they
remain with the Khan's other women in the palace,
where they are instructed in needle-work, glove-making,
and other elegant accomplishments. When some nobleman is looking for a wife, the Great Khan gives him one
of these damsels with a great dowry. And in this way he
marries them all off honourably.

You may be inclined to ask: 'Do not the men of this
province regard it as a grievance that the Great Khan robs
them of their daughters?' Most certainly not. They esteem
it a great favour and distinction; and those who have
beautiful daughters are delighted that he should deign to
accept them. They reason thus: 'If my daughter is born
under a good planet and happy auspices, the Khan will
be better able to satisfy her than I; he will marry her to a
noble husband, which is more than my means would
permit of.' And if she does not behave well or it does
not turn out well for her, then the father says: 'This has
happened to her because her planet was not propitious.'

You should know further that by his four wives the Great Khan has twenty-two male children. The eldest was called Chinghiz, for love of the good Chinghiz Khan. He was to have succeeded his father as Great Khan and lord of the whole empire. But it happened that he died, leaving a son named Temur; this Temur is now destined to be Great Khan and lord, because he is the son of the eldest son of the Great Khan. I can assure you that this Temur is a man of wisdom and prowess, as he has already proved many times on the field of battle.

By his mistresses the Great Khan has a further twenty-five sons, all good men and brave soldiers. And each of them is a great baron.

Of his sons by his four wives, seven are kings of great provinces and kingdoms. They all exercise their authority well, lacking neither prudence nor prowess. And for this there is good reason, for I give you my word that their father the Great Khan is the wisest man and the ablest in all respects, the best ruler of subjects and of empire and the man of the highest character of all that have ever been in the whole history of the Tartars.

You must know that for three months in the year, December, January, and February, the Great Khan lives in the capital city of Cathay, whose name is Khan-balik. In this city he has his great palace, which I will now describe to you.

The palace is completely surrounded by a square wall, each side being a mile in length so that the whole circuit is four miles. It is a very thick wall and fully ten paces in height. It is all whitewashed and battlemented. At each

corner of this wall stands a large palace of great beauty
and splendour, in which the Great Khan keeps his military stores. In the middle of each side is another palace
resembling the corner palaces, so that round the whole
circuit of the walls there are eight palaces, all serving
as arsenals. Each is reserved for a particular type of
munition. Thus, one contains saddles, bridles, stirrups,
and other items of a horse's harness. In another are
bows, bow-strings, quivers, arrows, and other requisites
of archery. In a third are cuirasses, corselets, and other
armour of boiled leather. And so with the rest.

In the southern front of this wall there are five gates.
There is one great gate in the middle, which is never
opened except when the Great Khan is leaving or entering. Next to this, one on either side, are two small gates,
by which everyone else enters. There are also two more
large gates, one near each corner, which are likewise
used by other people.

Within this outer wall is another wall, somewhat
greater in length than in breadth. In this also there are
eight palaces, just like the others, and used in the same
way to house military stores. It also has five gates in its
southern front, corresponding to those in the outer wall.
In each of the other sides it has one gate only; and so has
the outer wall.

Within this wall is the Great Khan's palace, which I
will now describe to you. It is the largest that was ever
seen. It has no upper floor, but the basement on which
it stands is raised ten palms above the level of the
surrounding earth; and all round it there runs a marble
wall level with the basement, two paces in thickness.

The foundation of the palace lies within this wall, so that as much of the wall as projects beyond it forms a sort of terrace, on which men can walk right round and inspect the outside of the palace. At the outer edge of this wall is a fine gallery with columns, where men can meet and talk. At each face of the palace is a great marble staircase, ascending from ground level to the top of this marble wall, which affords an entry into the palace.

The palace itself has a very high roof. Inside, the walls of the halls and chambers are all covered with gold and silver and decorated with pictures of dragons and birds and horsemen and various breeds of beasts and scenes of battle. The ceiling is similarly adorned, so that there is nothing to be seen anywhere but gold and pictures. The hall is so vast and so wide that a meal might well be served there for more than 6,000 men. The number of chambers is quite bewildering. The whole building is at once so immense and so well constructed that no man in the world, granted that he had the power to effect it, could imagine any improvement in design or execution. The roof is all ablaze with scarlet and green and blue and yellow and all the colours that are, so brilliantly varnished that it glitters like crystal and the sparkle of it can be seen from far away. And this roof is so strong and so stoutly built as to last for many a long year.

In the rear part of the palace are extensive apartments, both chambers and halls, in which are kept the private possessions of the Khan. Here is stored his treasure: gold, and silver, precious stones and pearls, and his gold and silver vessels. And here too are his ladies and his con-cubines. In these apartments everything is arranged for his comfort and convenience, and outsiders are not admitted.

Between the inner and the outer walls, of which I have told you, are stretches of park-land with stately trees. The grass grows here in abundance, because all the paths are paved and built up fully two cubits above the level of the ground, so that no mud forms on them and no rain-water collects in puddles, but the moisture trickles over the lawns, enriching the soil and promoting a lush growth of herbage. In these parks there is a great variety of game, such as white harts, musk-deer, roebuck, stags, squirrels, and many other beautiful animals. All the area within the walls is full of these graceful creatures, except the paths that people walk on.

In the north-western corner of the grounds is a pit of great size and depth, very neatly made, from which the earth was removed to build the mound of which I shall speak. The pit is filled with water by a fair-sized stream so as to form a sort of pond where the animals come to drink. The stream flows out through an aqueduct near the mound and fills another similar pit between the Great Khan's palace and that of Chinghiz his son, from which the earth was dug for the same purpose. These pits or ponds contain a great variety of fish. For the Great Khan has had them stocked with many different species, so that, whenever he feels inclined, he may have his pick. At the farther end of the pond there is an outlet for the stream, through which it flows away. It is so contrived that at the entrance and the outlet there are gratings of iron and copper to stop the fish from escaping. There are also swans and other water-fowl. It is possible to pass from one palace to the other by way of a bridge over this stream.

On the northern side of the palace, at the distance of a bow-shot but still within the walls, the Great Khan has had made an earthwork, that is to say a mound fully 100 paces in height and over a mile in circumference. This mound is covered with a dense growth of trees, all evergreens that never shed their leaves. And I assure you that whenever the Great Khan hears tell of a particularly fine tree he has it pulled up, roots and all and with a quantity of earth, and transported to this mound by elephants. No matter how big the tree may be, he is not deterred from transplanting it. In this way he has assembled here the finest trees in the world. In addition, he has had the mound covered with lapis lazuli, which is intensely green, so that trees and rock alike are as green as green can be and there is no other colour to be seen. For this reason it is called the Green Mound. On top of this mound, in the middle of the summit, he has a large and handsome palace, and this too is entirely green. And I give you my word that mound and trees and palace form a vision of such beauty that it gladdens the hearts of all beholders. It was for the sake of this entrancing view that the Great Khan had them constructed, as well as for the refreshment and recreation they might afford him.

Let me tell you also that beside this palace the Great Khan has had another one built, just like his own and no whit inferior. This is built to be occupied by his son when he shall succeed him as ruler. That is why it is built in the same style and on the same scale as the Great

Khan's own, which I have described above, and with walls of equal size. This is the residence of Temur the son of Chinghiz, of whom I have already spoken, who is destined to be Khan; and he observes the same ceremony and usages as the Great Khan, because he has been chosen to rule after the Great Khan's death. The bull and seal of empire are his already, though so long as the Great Khan is alive he does not enjoy them so absolutely.

Now that I have told you about these palaces, I will go on to tell you of the great town of Taidu in which they are situated, and why and how it came to be built.

On the banks of a great river in the province of Cathay there stood an ancient city of great size and splendour which was named Khan-balik, that is to say in our language 'the Lord's City'. Now the Great Khan discovered through his astrologers that this city would rebel and put up a stubborn resistance against the Empire. For this reason he had this new city built next to the old one, with only the river between. And he removed the inhabitants of the old city and settled them in the new one, which is called Taidu, leaving only those whom he did not suspect of any rebellious designs; for the new city was not big enough to house all those who lived in the old.

Taidu is built in the form of a square with all its sides of equal length and a total circumference of twenty-four miles. It is enclosed by earthern ramparts, twenty paces high and ten paces thick at the base; the sides slope inwards from base to summit, so that at the top the width is only about three paces. They are all battlemented and

white-washed. They have twelve gates, each sur-
mounted by a fine, large palace. So on each of the four
sides there are three gates and five palaces, because there
is an additional palace at each corner. In these palaces
there are immense halls, which house the weapons of
the city guards.

I assure you that the streets are so broad and straight
that from the top of the wall above one gate you can see
along the whole length of the road to the gate opposite.
The city is full of fine mansions, inns, and dwelling-
houses. All the way down the sides of every main street
there are booths and shops of every sort. All the building
sites throughout the city are square and measured by
the rule; and on every site stand large and spacious
mansions with ample courtyards and gardens. These
sites are allotted to heads of households, so that one
belongs to such-and-such a person, representing such-
and-such a family, the next to a representative of another
family, and so all the way along. Every site or block is
surrounded by good public roads; and in this way the
whole interior of the city is laid out in squares like a chess-
board with such masterly precision that no description
can do justice to it.

In this city there is such a multitude of houses and of
people, both within the walls and without, that no one
could count their number. Actually there are more
people outside the walls in the suburbs than in the city
itself. There is a suburb outside every gate, such that
each one touches the neighbouring suburbs on either
side. They extend in length for three or four miles. And
in every suburb or ward, at about a mile's distance from

the city, there are many fine hostels which provide lodging for merchants coming from different parts: a particular hostel is assigned to every nation, as we might say one for the Lombards, another for the Germans, another for the French. Merchants and others come here on business in great numbers, both because it is the Khan's residence and because it affords a profitable market. And the suburbs have as fine houses and mansions as the city, except of course for the Khan's palace.

You must know that no one who dies is buried in the city. If an idolater dies there, his body is taken to the place of cremation, which lies outside all the suburbs. And so with the others also; when they die they are taken right outside the suburbs for burial. Similarly, no act of violence is performed inside the city, but only outside the suburbs.

Let me tell you also that no sinful woman dares live within the city, unless it be in secret – no woman of the world, that is, who prostitutes her body for money. But they all live in the suburbs, and there are so many of them that no one could believe it. For I assure you that there are fully 20,000 of them, all serving the needs of men for money. They have a captain general, and there are chiefs of hundreds and of thousands responsible to the captain. This is because, whenever ambassadors come to the Great Khan on his business and are maintained at his expense, which is done on a lavish scale, the captain is called upon to provide one of these women every night for the ambassador and one for each of his attendants. They are changed every night and receive no payment; for this is the tax they pay to the Great Khan. From the number of these prostitutes you may infer the number of traders and other visitors who are daily coming and going here about their business.

You may take it for a fact that more precious and costly wares are imported into Khan-balik than into any other city in the world. Let me give you particulars. All the treasures that come from India – precious stones, pearls, and other rarities – are brought here. So too are the choicest and costliest products of Cathay itself and every other province. This is on account of the Great Khan himself, who lives here, and of the lords and ladies and the enormous multitude of hotel-keepers and other residents and of visitors who attend the courts held here by the Khan. That is why the volume and value of the imports and of the internal trade exceed those of any other city in the world. It is a fact that every day more than 1,000 cart-loads of silk enter the city; for much cloth of gold and silk is woven here. Furthermore, Khan-balik is surrounded by more than 200 other cities, near and far, from which traders come to it to sell and to buy. So it is not surprising that it is the centre of such a traffic as I have described.

In the centre of the city stands a huge palace in which is a great bell; in the evening this peals three times as a signal that no one may go about the town. Once this bell has sounded the due number of peals, no one ventures abroad in the city except in case of childbirth or illness; and those who are called out by such emergencies are obliged to carry lights. Every night there are guards riding about the city in troops of thirty or forty, to discover whether anyone is going about at an abnormal

hour, that is after the third peal of the bell. If anyone is
found, he is promptly arrested and clapped into prison.
Next morning he is examined by the officials appointed
for the purpose, and if he is found guilty of any offence, he
is punished according to its gravity with a proportionate
number of strokes of a rod, which sometimes cause
death. They employ this mode of punishment in order
to avoid bloodshed, because their *Bakhshi*, that is, the
adepts in astrology, declare that it is wrong to shed
human blood.

It is ordered that every gateway must be guarded by
1,000 men. You must not suppose that this guard is
maintained out of mistrust of the inhabitants. It is there,
in fact, partly as a mark of respect to the Great Khan
who lives in the city, partly as a check upon evil-doers –
although, because of the prophecy of his astrologers, the
Khan does harbour certain suspicions of the people of
Cathay.

Let me now tell you how on one occasion the Cathayans
in the city actually did plan to revolt. It is an established
practice, as will be explained below, that twelve men are
appointed with full powers of disposal over territories
and public offices at their own discretion. Among these
was a Saracen called Ahmad, a man of great energy and
ability, who surpassed all the rest in his authority and
influence over the Great Khan. The Emperor was so
fond of him that he gave him a completely free hand. It
seems, as was learnt after his death, that this Ahmad
used to bewitch the Emperor by his black arts to such
purpose that he won a ready hearing and acceptance for

everything he said; and so he was free to do whatever he chose. He used to make all appointments to office and punish all delinquents. Whenever he wished to cause the death of anyone whom he hated, whether justly or unjustly, he would go to the Emperor and say to him: 'So-and-so deserves to die, because he has offended your Majesty in such-and-such a way.' Then the Emperor would say: 'Do as you think best.' And Ahmad would thereupon put him to death. Therefore, seeing the complete liberty he enjoyed and the absolute faith reposed in him by the Emperor, men did not venture to thwart him in anything. There was no one so great or of such authority as not to fear him. If anyone was accused by him to the Emperor of a capital offence and wished to plead his cause, he had no chance to rebut the charge or state his own case, because he could count on no support – everyone was too much afraid of going against Ahmad. In this way, he caused the death of many innocent people.

Furthermore, there was not a pretty woman who took his fancy but he would have his will with her, taking her as a wife if she was not already married or otherwise enforcing her submission. Whenever he learnt that someone had a good-looking daughter, he would send his ruffians to the girl's father, and they would say: 'What is your ambition? Well then, how about this daughter of yours? Give her to the Bailo (for Ahmad was called by the title of Bailo or Lord-Lieutenant) and we will see that he gives you such-and-such a post or office for three years.' So the man would give him his daughter. Then Ahmad would say to the Khan: 'Such-and-such a post is vacant, or will fall vacant on such-and-such a date. So-and-so is the right man for the job.' To which the Khan would answer: 'Do as you think best.' And Ahmad would promptly instal him. By this means, playing partly on men's ambition for office, partly on their fears, Ahmad got possession of all the best-looking women as his wives and his concubines. He also had sons, some twenty-five of them, whom he installed in the highest offices. Some of them, under cover of their father's name, used to practise adultery in their father's fashion and commit many other crimes and abominations. Ahmad had also accumulated an immense fortune, because everyone who aspired to any post or office used to send him a handsome present.

Ahmad exercised this authority as governor for twenty-two years. At length the people of the country, that is the Cathayans, seeing that there was no end to the iniquities and abominations that he perpetrated beyond all measure at the expense of their womenfolk as well as their own persons, reached the point where they could endure it no longer. They made up their minds to assassinate him and revolt against the government of the city. Among their number was a Cathayan named Ch'ien-hu, a commander of 1,000, whose mother, daughter, and wife had all been ravished by Ahmad. Ch'ien-hu, moved by fierce indignation, plotted the destruction of the governor with another Cathayan named Wan-hu, a commander of 10,000.* They planned

---

* The titles *Ch'ien-hu* and *Wan-hu* mean respectively commander of 1,000 and of 10,000.

to do the deed when the Great Khan had completed his three months' sojourn at Khan-balik and had left for the city of Shang-tu, where he would likewise spend three months, and his son Chinghiz had also set out for his accustomed residences. At such times Ahmad was left to keep guard over the city: when the need arose, he would send word to the Great Khan at Shang-tu and the Khan would send back word of his wishes. The two plotters decided to impart their plot to the leading Cathayans of the country, and by common consent they made it known in many other cities to their own friends. The scheme was to take effect on the appointed day in the following manner. At the sight of a signal fire, all the conspirators were immediately to put to death any man wearing a beard and to pass on the signal to other cities by means of beacons that they should do the same. The reason for killing the bearded men was that the Cathayans are naturally beardless, whereas the Tartars, Saracens, and Christians wear beards. You must understand that all the Cathayans hated the government of the Great Khan, because he set over them Tartar rulers, mostly Saracens, and they could not endure it, since it made them feel that they were no more than slaves. Moreover the Great Khan had no legal title to rule the province of Cathay, having acquired it by force. So, putting no trust in the people, he committed the government of the country to Tartars, Saracens, and Christians who were attached to his household and personally loyal to him and not natives of Cathay.

Then Wan-hu and Ch'ien-hu, on the appointed date, entered the palace by night. And Wan-hu seated himself on the throne and had many lights lit in front of him. And he sent a courier to Ahmad, who lived in the old city, announcing that Chinghiz, the Khan's son, had just arrived that very night and summoned the Bailo to wait upon him without delay. When Ahmad heard this, he went immediately, greatly puzzled and not a little alarmed. On his way in through the city gate he met a Tartar named Kogatai, who was in command of the 12,000 men who kept constant watch and ward over the city. 'Where are you going at this late hour?' asked Kogatai. 'To Chinghiz, who has just arrived.' 'How is it possible,' asked Kogatai, 'that he can have arrived so secretly that I have heard nothing of it?' And he followed him with a detachment of his guard. Now the conspirators had said among themselves: 'If only we can kill Ahmad, we have nothing to fear from anything else.' The moment Ahmad entered the palace and saw it such a blaze of lights, he knelt before Wan-hu, mistaking him for Chinghiz; and Ch'ien-hu, who was there armed with a sword, cut off his head.

When Kogatai, who had stopped at the entrance to the palace, saw this, he shouted 'Treason!' And there and then he aimed an arrow at Wan-hu, who was seated on the throne, and shot him dead. Then, calling on his followers, he seized Ch'ien-hu. And he issued a proclamation throughout the city that anyone found out of doors would be killed on the spot. The Cathayans, seeing that the Tartars had discovered their plot and that they were left without a head, one of their leaders being killed and the other captured, stayed quietly in their homes and hence could give no sign to the other cities to carry out their plan of rebellion. Kogatai promptly sent couriers to the Great Khan with a full account of everything that had happened, and received in reply an order to conduct a thorough investigation and punish the guilty according to their deserts. When morning came, Kogatai examined all the Cathayans, and put to death many whom he found to be ring-leaders in the conspiracy. And the same thing was done in the other cities, when it came out that they were involved in the crime.

When the Great Khan had returned to Khan-balik, he wanted to know the cause of this occurrence. He then learnt the truth about the abominable outrages committed, as already related, by the execrable Ahmad and his sons. He found out that Ahmad himself and seven of his sons – for they were not all wicked – had taken innumerable ladies to be their wives, not to speak of those whom they had possessed by force. Then he caused all the treasure that Ahmad had amassed in the Old City to be brought into the New City; and put it with his own treasure; and it was found to be beyond all reckoning. He ordered Ahmad's body to be taken from the grave and flung in the street to be torn to pieces by dogs. And those of his sons who had followed the example of his evil deeds he caused to be flayed alive. And when he called to mind the accursed doctrine of the Saracens, by which every sin is accounted a lawful act even to the killing of any man who is not of their creed, so that because of it the execrable Ahmad and his sons were not conscious of committing any sin, he utterly contemned it and held it in abomination. He summoned the Saracens to his presence and expressly forbade them to do many things which their law commanded. In particular he commanded them to take their wives according to the law of the Tartars and not to cut the throats of animals, as they used to do, in order to eat their flesh, but to slit their bellies. And at the time when all this happened, Messer Marco was in this place.

As for the Great Khan's guard of 12,000 men, you must know that they are called *Keshikten*, which is as much as to say 'knights and liegemen of the lord'. He employs them not out of fear of any man but in token of his sovereignty. These 12,000 horsemen have four captains, one over every 3,000. Each 3,000 in turn reside in the Khan's palace for three days and three nights and eat and drink there, and at the end of that time another 3,000 take their place, and so they continue throughout the year. By day indeed the other 9,000 do not leave the palace, unless it happens that one of them goes off on the Khan's affairs or on some urgent private business and then only if it is legitimate and he has his captain's leave. If he is faced with something really serious, such as the impending death of a father or brother or other near relative, or the threat of some heavy loss which would not permit of his immediate return, then he must get leave from the Khan. But at night the 9,000 are free to go home.

When the Great Khan is holding court, the seating at banquets is arranged as follows. He himself sits at a much higher table than the rest at the northern end of the hall, so that he faces south. His principal wife sits next to him on the left. On the right, at a somewhat lower level, sit his sons in order of age, Chinghiz the eldest being placed rather higher than the rest, and his grandsons and his kinsmen of the imperial lineage. They are so placed that their heads are on a level with the Great Khan's feet. Next to them are seated the other noblemen at other tables lower down again. And the ladies are seated on the same plan. All the wives of the Khan's sons and grandsons and kinsmen are seated on his left at a lower level, and next to them the wives of his nobles and knights lower down still. And they all know their appointed place in the lord's plan. The tables are so arranged that the Great Khan can see everything, and there are a great many of them. But you must not imagine that all the guests sit at table; for most of the knights and nobles in the hall take their meal seated on carpets for want of tables. Outside the hall the guests at the banquet number more than 40,000. For they include many visitors with costly gifts, men who come from strange countries bringing strange things, and some who have held high office and aspire to further advancement. Such are the guests who attend on such occasions, when the Great Khan is holding court or celebrating a wedding.

In the midst of the hall where the Great Khan has his table is a very fine piece of furniture of great size and splendour in the form of a square chest, each side being three paces in length, elaborately carved with figures of animals finely wrought in gold. The inside is hollow and contains a huge golden vessel in the form of a pitcher with the capacity of a butt, which is filled with wine. In each corner of the chest is a vessel with the capacity of a firkin, one filled with mares' milk, one with camels' milk, and the others with other beverages. On the chest stand all the Khan's vessels in which drink is served to him. From it the wine or other precious beverage is drawn off to fill huge stoups of gold, each containing enough to satisfy eight or ten men. One of these is set between every two men seated at the table. Each of the two has a gold cup with a handle, which he fills from the stoup. And for every pair of ladies one stoup and two cups are provided in the same way. You must understand that these stoups and the rest are of great value. I can assure you that the Great Khan has such a store of vessels of gold and silver that no one who did not see it with his own eyes could well believe it. And the waiters who serve his food and drink are certain of his barons. They have their mouths and noses swathed in fine napkins of silk and gold, so that the food and drink are not contaminated by their breath or effluence.

Certain barons are also appointed to look after new-comers unfamiliar with court etiquette and show them to their allotted and appropriate seats. These barons are continually passing to and fro through the hall, asking the guests if they lack anything. And if there are any who want wine or milk or anything else, they have it promptly brought to them by the waiters. At all the entrances of the hall, or wherever else the Great Khan may be, stand two men of gigantic stature, one on either side, with staves in their hands. This is because it is not permissible for anyone to touch the threshold of the door, but all who enter must step over it. If anyone should happen to touch it by accident, the guardians take his clothes from him and he must pay a fine to redeem them. Or if they do not take his clothes, they administer the appointed number of blows. But if they are newcomers who do not know of the rule, certain barons are assigned to introduce them and warn them of the rule. This is done because touching the threshold is looked upon as a bad omen. In leaving the hall, since some of the guests are overcome with drinking so that they could not possibly exercise due care, no such rule is enjoined.

There are many instruments in the hall, of every sort, and when the Great Khan is about to drink they all strike up. As soon as the cup-bearer has handed him the cup, he retires three paces and kneels down; and all the barons and all the people present go down on their knees and make a show of great humility. Then the Great Khan drinks. And every time he drinks the same performance is repeated. Of the food I say nothing, because everyone will readily believe that there is no lack of it. Let me add that there is no baron or knight at the banquet but brings his wife to dine with the other ladies. When they have fed and the tables are removed, a great troupe of jugglers and acrobats and other entertainers comes into the hall and performs remarkable feats of various kinds. And they all afford great amusement and entertainment in the Khan's presence, and the guests show their enjoyment by peals of laughter. When all is over, the guests take their leave and return each to his own lodging or house.

You must know that all the Tartars celebrate their birthdays as festivals. The Great Khan was born on the twenty-eighth day of the lunar cycle in the month of September. And on this day he holds the greatest feast of the year, excepting only the new year festival of which

I will tell you later. On his birthday he dons a magnificent robe of beaten gold. And fully 12,000 barons and knights robe themselves with him in a similar colour and style – not so costly as his, but still of the same colour and style, in cloth of silk and gold, and all with gold belts. These robes are given to them by the Great Khan. And I assure you that the value of some of these robes, reckoning the precious stones and pearls with which they are often adorned, amounts to 10,000 golden bezants. Of such there are not a few. And you must know that the Great Khan gives rich robes to these 12,000 barons and knights thirteen times a year, so that they are all dressed in robes like his own and of great value. You can see for yourselves that this is no light matter, and that there is no other prince in the world besides himself who could bear such an expense.

On this royal birthday all the Tartars in the world, all the provinces and regions where men hold land and lordship under the Great Khan, give him costly presents proportionate to the giver and in accordance with prescribed order. And rich gifts are also brought to him by many others, petitioners for high office – which is awarded to applicants according to merit by twelve barons appointed for the purpose. And on this day all the idolaters and all the Christians and all the Saracens and all the races of men offer solemn prayers to their idols and their gods, with singing of hymns and lighting of lamps and burning of incense, that they may save their lord and give him long life and joy and health. So this day is passed in merry-making and birthday festivities. Now that I have fully described them, let us turn to another great feast which is celebrated at the new year and is called the White Feast.

The new year begins with them in February, and this is how it is observed by the Great Khan and all his subjects. According to custom they all array themselves in white, both male and female, so far as their means allow. And this they do because they regard white costume as auspicious and benign, and they don it at the new year so that throughout the year they may enjoy prosperity and happiness. On this day all the rulers, and all the provinces and regions and realms where men hold land or lordship under his sway, bring him costly gifts of gold and silver and pearls and precious stones and abundance of fine white cloth, so that throughout the year their lord may have no lack of treasure and may live in joy and gladness. Let me tell you also that the barons and knights and all the people make gifts to one another of white things. And they greet one another gaily and cheerfully saying, very much as we do: 'May this year be a lucky one for you and bring you success in all you undertake.' And this they do so that throughout the year all may go well with them and all their enterprises prosper.

I can also assure you for a fact that on this day the Great Khan receives gifts of more than 100,000 white horses, of great beauty and price. And on this day also there is a procession of his elephants, fully 5,000 in number, all draped in fine cloths embroidered with beasts and birds. Each one bears on its back two strong-boxes of great beauty and price filled with the Khan's plate and with costly apparel for this white-robed court. With them come innumerable camels also draped with cloths and laden with provisions for the feast. They all defile in front of the Great Khan and it is the most splendid sight that ever was seen.

On the morning of this feast, before the tables are set up, all the kings and all the dukes, marquises and counts, barons, knights, astrologers, physicians, falconers, and many other officials and rulers of men and lands and armies appear before the Khan in the great hall. And those who do not achieve this assemble outside the palace in a spot where the Khan can readily inspect them. Let me tell you in what order they are stationed. In front are his sons and grandsons and those of his imperial lineage. Next come the kings, then the dukes and then all the other ranks, one behind another, in due order. And when they are all seated, each in his proper station, up stands a great dignitary and proclaims in a loud voice: 'Bow down and worship!' No sooner has he said this than they bow down, then and there, and touch the ground with their foreheads, and address a prayer to the lord and worship him as if he were a god. Then the dignitary proclaims: 'God save our lord and long preserve him in gladness and joy!' And one and all reply: 'God do so!' Once again the dignitary proclaims: 'God increase and multiply his empire from good to better and keep all his subjects in untroubled peace and good will and in all his lands grant universal prosperity!' And one and all reply: 'God do so!' In this manner they worship him four times. Then they go to an altar, adorned with great splendour, on which is a scarlet tablet bearing the name of the Great Khan, and also a splendidly wrought censer.

They cense this tablet and the altar with great reverence. Then they return, each to his place. When they have all done this, then the precious gifts of which I have spoken are presented. After this, when the Great Khan has viewed all the gifts, the tables are laid and the guests take their places in due order as I have already related – the Khan alone at his high table with his first wife, and the others each in his degree, and their ladies on the empress's side of the hall, just as I have described it to you before. When they have fed, the performers come in and entertain the court as before. Finally they return, everyone to his own lodging or home.

Next let me tell you that the Great Khan has ordained thirteen feasts, one for each of the thirteen lunar months, which are attended by the 12,000 barons called *Keshikten*, that is to say the henchmen most closely attached to the Khan. To each of these he has given thirteen robes, every one of a different colour. They are splendidly adorned with pearls and gems and other ornaments and are of immense value. He has also given to each of the 12,000 a gold belt of great beauty and price, and shoes of fine leather (called *canaut* or *borgal*) cunningly embroidered with silver thread, which are likewise beautiful and costly. All their attire is so gorgeous and so stately that when they are fully robed any one of them might pass for a king. One of these robes is appointed to be worn at each of the thirteen feasts. The Great Khan himself has thirteen similar robes – similar, that is, in colour, but more splendid and costly and more richly adorned; and he always dresses in the same colour as his barons.

The cost of these robes, to the number of 156,000 in

all, amounts to a quantity of treasure that is almost past computation, to say nothing of the belts and shoes, which also cost a goodly sum. And all this the Khan does for the embellishment or enhancement of his feasts.

Let me conclude with one more fact, a very remarkable one well worthy of mention in our book. You must know that a great lion is led into the Great Khan's presence; and as soon as it sees him it flings itself down prostrate before him with every appearance of deep humility and seems to acknowledge him as lord. There it stays without a chain, and is indeed a thing to marvel at.

We will turn next to the Great Khan's hunting parties.

You may take it for a fact that during the three months which the Great Khan spends in the city of Khan-balik, that is, December, January, and February, he has ordered that within a distance of sixty days' journey from where he is staying everybody must devote himself to hunting and hawking. The order goes out to every governor of men or lands to send all such large beasts as wild boars, harts, stags, roebucks, bears, and the like, or at any rate the greater part of them. So every governor gathers round him all the huntsmen of the district, and together they go wherever these beasts are to be found, beating their coverts in turn and killing some of them with their hounds but most with their arrows. That is how they hunt them. And those beasts that they wish to send to the Great Khan they first disembowel and then load on carts and so dispatch. This applies to all those within thirty days' journey, and their combined bag is enormous. Those distant from thirty to sixty days do not send the flesh – the journey is too long for that – but send the hides duly dressed and tanned, so that the Khan may use them in the manufacture of necessary equipment for his armies.

You must know also that the Great Khan has a plentiful supply of leopards skilled in hunting game and of lynxes trained in the chase and past masters of their craft. He has a number of lions of immense size, bigger than those of Egypt; they have very handsome, richly coloured fur, with longitudinal stripes of black, orange, and white. They are trained to hunt wild boars and bulls, bears, wild asses, stags, roebuck, and other game. A grand sight it is to see the stately creatures that fall a prey to these lions. When the lions are led out to the chase, they are carried on carts in cages, each with a little dog for company. They are caged because otherwise they would be too ferocious and too eager in their pursuit of game, so that there would be no holding them. They must always be led upwind; for if their prey caught wind of the smell they would not wait, but would be off in a flash. He has also a great many eagles trained to take wolves and foxes and fallow-deer and roe-deer, and these too bring in game in plenty. Those that are trained to take wolves are of immense size and power, for there is never a wolf so big that he escapes capture by one of these eagles.

Now that you have heard what I have to tell on this subject, I will tell you of the numbers and excellence of the Great Khan's hounds. You must know that among his barons there are two brothers in blood who are named Bayan and Mingan. They bear the title *kuyukchi*, that is to say, keepers of the mastiffs. Each of them has 10,000 subordinates, who all wear livery of one colour; and the other 10,000 all wear another colour. The two colours are scarlet and blue. Whenever they accompany the Great Khan in the chase, they wear these liveries. Among either 10,000 there are 2,000 of whom each one leads a mastiff, or maybe two or more, so that the total number is immense. When the Great Khan goes hunting, one of the two brothers with his 10,000 men and fully 5,000 hounds goes with him on one side and the other with his 10,000 and his hounds goes on the other. The two bands keep pace with each other exactly, so that the whole line extends in length over a day's journey. And not a wild beast do they find but falls a prey. What a sight it is to see the hunt and the performance of the hounds and the hunters! For you must picture that, while the Great Khan rides out hawking with his barons across the open country, then packs of these hounds are to be seen advancing on either side, hunting bears and stags and other beasts, so that it is truly a fine sight to see. These two brothers are bound by covenant to provide the Great Khan's court every day, beginning in October and continuing to the end of March, with a thousand head of game, including both beasts and birds, except quails, and also fish to the best of their ability, reckoning as the equivalent of one head as much fish as would make a square meal for three persons.

When the Khan has spent the three months of December, January, and February in the city of which I have spoken, he sets off in March and travels south-ward to within two days' journey of the Ocean. He is accompanied by fully 10,000 falconers and takes with him fully 5,000 gerfalcons and peregrine falcons and sakers in great abundance, besides a quantity of goshawks for hawking along the riversides. You must not imagine that he keeps all this company with him in one place. In fact he distributes them here and there, in groups of a hundred or two hundred or more. Then they engage in fowling, and most of the fowl they take are brought to the Great Khan. And I would have you know that when he goes hawking with his gerfalcons and other hawks, he has fully 10,000 men in parties of two who are called *toscaor*, which signifies in our language 'watchmen'. These men are posted here and there in couples, so as to occupy a wide enough area. Each has a call and a hood, so that they can call in the hawks and hold them. And when the Khan orders the hawks to be cast, there is no need for the casters to go after them, because the men of whom I have spoken, dispersed here and there, keep such careful watch that wherever a hawk may go they are always on the spot and if one is in need of help they are prompt to render it.

All the Great Khan's hawks and those of the other barons have a little tablet of silver attached to their feet on which is written the name of the owner and also that of the keeper. By this means the bird is recognized as soon as it is taken, and is returned to the owner. If the finder does not know whose it is, he takes it to a baron who is called *bularguchi*, which is as much as to say 'keeper of lost property'. For, I would have you know that, if anyone finds a horse or a sword or a hawk or anything else and cannot discover the owner, it is immediately brought to this baron, and he takes charge of it. If the finder does not hand it over forthwith, he is reckoned a thief. And the losers apply to this baron, and if he has received their property he promptly returns it. He always has his official residence, with its flag flying, at the highest point in the whole camp, so as to be readily seen by those who have lost anything. By this means nothing can be lost without being found and returned.

When the Great Khan goes on the journey of which I have told you towards the Ocean, the expedition is marked by many fine displays of huntsmanship and falconry. Indeed, there is no sport in the world to compare with it. He always rides on the back of four elephants, in a very handsome shelter of wood, covered inside with cloth of beaten gold and outside with lionskins. Here he always keeps twelve gerfalcons of the best he possesses and is attended by several barons to entertain him and keep him company. When he is travelling in this shelter on the elephants, and other barons who are riding in his train call out, 'Sire, there are cranes passing,' and he orders the roof of the shelter to be thrown open and so sees the cranes, he bids his attendants fetch such gerfalcons as he may choose and lets them fly. And often, the gerfalcons take the cranes in full view while the Great Khan remains all the while on his couch. And this affords him great sport and recreation. Meanwhile the other barons and knights ride all round him. And you may rest assured that there never was, and I do not believe there ever will be, any man who can enjoy such sport and recreation in this world as he does, or has such facilities for doing so.

When he has travelled so far that he arrives at a place called Cachar Modun, then he finds his pavilions ready pitched there and those of his sons and his barons and his mistresses to the number of more than 10,000; and very fine they are, and very costly. Let me tell you how his pavilion is made. First, the tent in which he holds his court is big enough to accommodate fully a thousand knights. This tent has its entrance towards the south and serves as a hall for the barons and other retainers. Adjoining this is another tent which faces west and is occupied by the Khan himself. It is to this tent that he summons anyone with whom he wishes to converse. At the back of the great hall is a large and handsome chamber in which he sleeps. There are also other chambers and other tents; but they do not adjoin the great tent. Let me tell you how these two halls and the chamber are constructed. Each hall has columns of spicewood very skilfully carved. On the outside they are all covered with lion-skins of great beauty, striped with black and white and orange. They are so well designed that neither wind nor rain can harm them or do any mischief. Inside they are all of ermine and sable, which are the two finest and richest and costliest furs there are. The truth is that a superfine sable fur big enough for a man's cloak is worth up to 2,000 golden bezants, while an ordinary one is worth 1,000. The Tartars call it 'the king of furs'. The sable is about the size of a marten. With these two sorts of skin the two great halls are lined, pieced together with such artistry that it is a truly amazing spectacle. And the chamber where the Khan sleeps, which adjoins the two halls, is also of lion-skins without and ermine and sable within, magnificent in workmanship and design. The cords that hold up the halls and chambers are all of silk. So precious indeed and so costly are these three tents that no petty king could afford them.

Round these three tents are pitched all the other tents, also well designed and appointed. The Khan's mistresses too have splendid pavilions. And for the gerfalcons and falcons and other birds and beasts there are tents in vast numbers. What need of more words? You may take it for a fact that the number of people in this camp almost passes belief. You might well fancy that the Khan was here in residence in his finest city. For it is thronged with multitudes from all parts. His whole household staff is here with him, besides physicians and astrologers and falconers and other officials in great numbers, and everything is as well ordered as in his capital.

In this place he stays till spring, which in these parts falls about our Easter Day. Throughout his stay he never ceases to go hawking by lake or stream, and he makes an ample catch of cranes and swans and other birds. And his followers who are dispersed about the neighbourhood send in lavish contributions of game and fowl. All this time he enjoys the finest sport and recreation in the world, so that no one in the world who has not seen it could ever believe it; so far do his magnificence and his state and his pleasures surpass my description.

Let me tell you one thing more. No merchant or artisan or peasant dare keep any falcon or bird of prey or any hound for the chase within twenty days' journey of the Great Khan's residence; but in every other province and region of his dominions they are free to hunt and do as they please with hawks and hounds. And you must understand, furthermore, that throughout his empire no king or baron or any other person dares to take or hunt hare or hart, buck or stag, or any other such beast between the months of March and October, so that they may increase and multiply. And anyone who contravenes this rule is made to repent it bitterly, because it is the Khan's own enactment. And I assure you that his commandment is so strictly obeyed that hares and bucks and the other beasts I have mentioned often come right up to a man, and he does not touch them or do them any harm.

After spending his time here in this fashion till about Easter Day, the Great Khan sets out with all his retainers and returns direct to the city of Khan-balik by the same route by which he came, hunting and hawking all the way and enjoying good sport.

It is in this city of Khan-balik that the Great Khan has his mint; and it is so organized that you might well say that he has mastered the art of alchemy. I will demonstrate this to you here and now.

You must know that he has money made for him by the following process, out of the bark of trees – to be precise, from mulberry trees (the same whose leaves furnish food for silkworms). The fine bast between the bark and the wood of the tree is stripped off. Then it is crumbled and pounded and flattened out with the aid of glue into sheets like sheets of cotton paper, which are all black. When made, they are cut up into rectangles of various sizes, longer than they are broad. The smallest is worth half a small tornesel; the next an entire such tornesel; the next half a silver groat; the next an entire silver groat, equal in value to a silver groat of Venice; and there are others equivalent to two, five, and ten groats and one, three, and as many as ten gold bezants. And all these papers are sealed with the seal of the Great Khan. The procedure of issue is as formal and as authoritative as if they were made of pure gold or silver. On each piece of money several specially appointed officials write their names, each setting his own stamp. When it is completed in due form, the chief of the officials deputed by the Khan dips in cinnabar the seal or bull assigned to him and stamps it on the top of the piece of money so that the shape of the seal in vermilion remains impressed upon it. And then the money is authentic. And if anyone were to forge it, he would suffer the extreme penalty.

Of this money the Khan has such a quantity made that with it he could buy all the treasure in the world. With this currency he orders all payments to be made throughout every province and kingdom and region of his empire. And no one dares refuse it on pain of losing his life. And I assure you that all the peoples and populations who are subject to his rule are perfectly willing to accept these papers in payment, since wherever they go they pay in the same currency, whether for goods or for pearls or precious stones or gold or silver. With these pieces of paper they can buy anything and pay for anything. And I can tell you that the papers that reckon as ten bezants do not weigh one.

Several times a year parties of traders arrive with

pearls and precious stones and gold and silver and other valuables, such as cloth of gold and silk, and surrender them all to the Great Khan. The Khan then summons twelve experts, who are chosen for the task and have special knowledge of it, and bids them examine the wares that the traders have brought and pay for them what they judge to be their true value. The twelve experts duly examine the wares and pay the value in the paper currency of which I have spoken. The traders accept it willingly, because they can spend it afterwards on the various goods they buy throughout the Great Khan's dominions. And I give you my word that the wares brought in at different times during the year mount up to a value of fully 400,000 bezants, and they are all paid for in this paper currency.

Let me tell you further that several times a year a fiat goes forth through the towns that all those who have gems and pearls and gold and silver must bring them to the Great Khan's mint. This they do, and in such abundance that it is past all reckoning; and they are all paid in paper money. By this means the Great Khan acquires all the gold and silver and pearls and precious stones of all his territories.

Here is another fact well worth relating. When these papers have been so long in circulation that they are growing torn and frayed, they are brought to the mint and changed for new and fresh ones at a discount of 3 per cent. And here again is an admirable practice that well deserves mention in our book: if a man wants to buy gold or silver to make his service of plate or his belts or other finery, he goes to the Khan's mint with some of these papers and gives them in payment for the gold and silver which he buys from the mint-master. And all the Khan's armies are paid with this sort of money.

I have now told you how it comes about that the Great Khan must have, as indeed he has, more treasure than anyone else in the world. I may go further and affirm that all the world's great potentates put together have not such riches as belong to the Great Khan alone.

Let me tell you next of the magnates who exercise authority from Khan-balik.

You must know that the Great Khan, as already mentioned, has appointed twelve great and powerful barons to supervise all decisions concerning the movement of the armies, changes in the high command, and dispatch of troops to one theatre or another in greater or less force, as need may require, according to the importance of the war. In addition it rests with them to sort out the staunch and fearless fighters from the faint-hearted, promoting the former and degrading those who prove incompetent or cowardly. And if anyone is captain of a thousand and has disgraced himself in any action, these barons decide that he has shown himself unworthy of his office and debase him to the rank of captain of a hundred. But if he has conducted himself creditably and with distinction, so that they judge him fit for a higher command, they advance him to a captaincy of ten thousand. In every case, however, they act with the knowledge of the Great Khan. When they propose to degrade anyone, they say to the Khan, 'So-and-so is unworthy of such-and-such an office,' to which he replies, 'Let him be degraded to a lower rank'; and so it is done. If they have it in mind to promote anyone in acknowledgement of his merits, they say, 'Such-and-such a captain of a thousand is fit and worthy to be captain of ten thousand'; then the Khan confirms the appointment and gives him the appropriate tablet, as previously described, and immediately orders him to be given presents of great value, so as to encourage the others to make the most of their abilities. This council of twelve barons is called *Thai*, that is to say 'Supreme Court', because there is no higher authority except the Great Khan himself.

Besides these there are twelve other barons to whom the Khan has committed authority over all the affairs of the thirty-four provinces. And this is how they are organized. Let me tell you first that they live in a palace in the town of Khan-balik, a palace of great size and beauty with many halls and residential quarters. For every province there is a judge and a staff of clerks, who all live in this palace, each in his own private residence. And the judge and his staff administer all the affairs of the province to which they are assigned, subject to the will and authority of the twelve barons. It rests with these barons to choose the governors of all the provinces. And when they have chosen men whom they consider competent and suitable, they recommend them to the Great Khan, who confirms their appointment and confers the appropriate tablet. They also supervise the collection of taxes and revenues together with their administration and expenditure and all else that concerns the imperial government throughout these provinces, except purely military matters. This Council goes by the name of *Shieng*, and the palace in which it is housed is also called *Shieng*.

Both the Thai and the Shieng are supreme courts, having no authority above them except the Great Khan himself, and enjoying the power to confer great benefits on whom they will. The Thai, however, that is to say the military court, is esteemed more highly and carries greater dignity than any other office.

I do not propose to enumerate the provinces at this stage, as I shall be giving a full account of them later in the book. Let us turn now to the system of post-horses by which the Great Khan sends his dispatches.

You must know that the city of Khan-balik is a centre from which many roads radiate to many provinces, one to each, and every road bears the name of the province to which it runs. The whole system is admirably contrived. When one of the Great Khan's messengers sets out along any of these roads, he has only to go twenty-five miles and there he finds a posting station, which in their language is called *yamb* and in our language may be rendered 'horse post'. At every post the messengers find a spacious and palatial hostelry for their lodging. These hostelries have splendid beds with rich coverlets of silk and all that befits an emissary of high rank. If a king came here, he would be well lodged. Here the messengers find no less than 400 horses, stationed here by the Great Khan's orders and always kept in readiness for his messengers when they are sent on any mission. And you must understand that posts such as these, at distances of twenty-five or thirty miles, are to be found along all the main highways leading to the provinces of which I have spoken. And at each of these posts the messengers find three or four hundred horses in readiness awaiting their command, and palatial lodgings such as I have described. And this holds good throughout all the provinces and kingdoms of the Great Khan's empire.

When the messengers are travelling through out-of-the-way country, where there are no homesteads or habitations, they find that the Great Khan has had posts established even in these wilds, with the same palatial accommodation and the same supply of horses and accoutrements. But here the stages are longer; for the posts are thirty-five miles apart and in some cases over forty miles.

By this means the Great Khan's messengers travel throughout his dominions and have lodgings and horses fully accoutred for every stage. And this is surely the highest privilege and the greatest resource ever enjoyed by any man on earth, king or emperor or what you will. For you may be well assured that more than 200,000 horses are stabled at these posts for the special use of these messengers. Moreover, the posts themselves number more than 10,000, all furnished on the same lavish scale. The whole organization is so stupendous and so costly that it baffles speech and writing.

If anyone is puzzled to understand how there can be enough people to execute such tasks, and what is the source of their livelihood, my answer is this. All the idolaters, and likewise the Saracens, take six, eight, or ten wives apiece, as many as they can afford to keep, and beget innumerable children. Hence there will be many men with more than thirty sons of their own, who all follow them under arms. This follows from the plurality of wives. With us, on the other hand, a man has only one wife, and if she should prove barren he will end his days with her and beget no children. Hence our population is less than theirs. As to the means of life, they have no shortage, because they mostly use rice, panic, or millet, especially the Tartars and the people of Cathay and Manzi, and these three cereals in their countries yield an increase of a hundredfold on each sowing. These peoples do not use bread, but simply boil these three sorts of grain with milk or flesh and then eat them. Wheat in their country does not yield such an increase; but such of it as they harvest they eat only in the form of noodles or other pasty foods. Among them no land is left idle that might be cultivated. Their beasts increase and multiply without end. When they are on military service, there is not one of them who does not lead with him six, eight, or more horses for his own use. So it is not difficult to understand why the population in these parts is so enormous and the means of life so plentiful.

Now let me tell you another thing which I forgot to mention – one that is very germane to the matter in hand. The fact is that between one post and the next, at distances of three miles apart, there are stations which may contain as many as forty buildings occupied by unmounted couriers, who also play a part in the Great Khan's postal service. I will tell you how. They wear large belts, set all round with bells, so that when they run they are audible at a great distance. They always run at full speed and never for more than three miles. And at the next station three miles away, where the noise they make gives due notice of their approach, another courier is waiting in readiness. As soon as the first man arrives, the new one takes what he is carrying and also a little note given to him by the clerk, and starts to run. After he has run for three miles, the performance is repeated. And I can assure you that by means of this service of unmounted couriers, the Great Khan receives news over a ten days' journey in a day and a night. For it takes these runners no more than a day and a night to cover a ten days' journey, or two days and two nights for a twenty days' journey. So in ten days they can transmit news over a journey of a hundred days. And in the fruit season it often happens that by this means fruit gathered in the morning in the city of Khan-balik is delivered on the evening of the next day to the Great Khan in the city of Shang-tu, ten days' journey away.

At each of these three-mile stations there is appointed a clerk who notes the day and hour of the arrival of every courier and the departure of his successor; and this practice is in force at every station. And there are also inspectors charged with the duty of going round every month and examining all these stations, in order to detect any couriers who have been remiss and punish them. From these couriers, and from the staff at the stations, the Great Khan exacts no tax, and he makes generous provision for their maintenance.

As for the horses of which I have spoken, which are kept in such numbers at the posts to carry the imperial messengers, I will tell you exactly how the Great Khan has established them. First he inquires, 'Which is the nearest city to such-and-such a post?'; then, 'How many horses can it maintain for the messengers?' Then the civic authorities investigate by means of experts how many horses can be maintained in the neighbouring post by the city and how many by the local towns and villages, and they apportion them according to the resources available. The cities act in concert, taking into consideration that between one post and the next there is sometimes another city, which makes its contribution with the rest. They provide for the horses out of the taxes due to the Great Khan: thus, if a man is assessed for taxation at a sum that would maintain a horse and a half, he is ordered to make corresponding provision at the neighbouring post. But you must understand that the cities do not maintain 400 horses continuously at each post. Actually they keep 200 for a month, to sustain the burdens of the post, while the other 200 are fattening. At the end of the month the fattened horses are transferred to the post while the others take their turn at grass. So they alternate perpetually.

If it happens at any point that there is some river or lake over which the couriers and mounted messengers must pass, the neighbouring cities keep three or four ferry-boats continually in readiness for this purpose. And if there is a desert to cross of many days' journey in extent, in which no permanent habitation can be established, the city next to the desert is obliged to furnish horses to the Khan's envoys to see them across, together with provisions for their escort. But to such cities the Khan affords special aid. And in out-of-the-way posts the horses are maintained partly by the Khan himself, partly by the nearest cities, towns, and villages.

When the need arises for the Great Khan to receive immediate tidings by mounted messenger, as of the rebellion of a subject country or of one of his barons or any matter that may concern him deeply, I assure you that the messengers ride 200 miles in a day, sometimes even 250. Let me explain how it is done. When a messenger wishes to travel at this speed and cover so many miles in a day, he carries a tablet with the sign of the gerfalcon as a token that he wishes to ride post haste. If there are two of them, they set out from the place where they are on two good horses, strongly built and swift runners. They tighten their belts and swathe their heads and off they go with all the speed they can muster, till they reach the next post-house twenty-five miles away. As they draw near they sound a sort of horn which is audible at a great distance, so that horses may be got ready for them. On arrival they find two fresh horses, ready harnessed, fully rested, and in good running form. They mount there and then, without a moment's breathing-space, and are no sooner mounted than off they go again, taking the last ounce out of their horses and not pausing till they reach the next post, where they find two more horses harnessed as before. Then up and off again. And so it goes on till evening. That is how these messengers manage to cover 250 miles a day with news for the Great Khan. Indeed, in extreme urgency, they can achieve 300 miles. In such cases they ride all night long; and if there is no moon the men of the post run in front of them with torches as far as the next post. But they cannot ride as fast by night as by day, because they are delayed by the slower pace of the runners. Messengers who can endure the fatigue of such a ride as this are very highly prized.

Now let me tell you something of the bounties that the Great Khan confers upon his subjects. For all his thoughts are directed towards helping the people who are subject to him, so that they may live and labour and increase their wealth. You may take it for a fact that he sends emissaries and inspectors throughout all his dominions and kingdoms and provinces to learn whether any of his people have suffered a failure of their crops either through weather or through locusts or other pests. And if he finds that any have lost their harvest, he exempts them for that year from their tribute and even gives them some of his own grain to sow and to eat – a magnificent act of royal bounty. This he does in the summer. And in winter he does likewise in the matter of cattle. If he finds any man whose cattle have been killed by an outbreak of plague, he gives him some of his own, derived from the tithes of other provinces, and to help him further he relieves him of tribute for the year.

Again, if it should happen that lightning strikes any flock of sheep or herd of other beasts, whether the herd belongs to one person or more and no matter how big it may be, the Great Khan will not take tithe of it for three years. And similarly if it chances to strike a ship laden with merchandise, he will not have any due or share of the cargo, because he accounts it an ill omen when lightning strikes any man's possessions. He reasons: 'God must have been angry with this man, since He launched a thunderbolt at him.' Therefore he does not wish that such possessions, struck by the wrath of God, should find their way into his treasury.

Here is another benefit that he confers.

Along the main highways frequented by his messengers and by merchants and other folk, he has ordered trees to be planted on both sides, two paces distant from one another. They are so large that they can be seen from a long way off. And he has done this so that any wayfarer may recognize the roads and not lose his way. For you will find these wayside trees in the heart of the wilderness; and a great boon they are to travellers and traders. They extend throughout every province and every kingdom. Where the roads traverse sandy deserts or rocky mountain ranges, so that it is not possible to plant trees, he has other land-marks set up in the form of cairns or pillars to indicate the track. He has certain officials whose duty it is to ensure that these are always kept in order. Besides the reasons already mentioned, he is all the more willing to have these trees planted because his soothsayers and astrologers declare that he who causes trees to be planted lives long.

You must know that most of the inhabitants of the province of Cathay drink a wine such as I will describe to you. They make a drink of rice and an assortment of excellent spices, prepared in such a way that it is better to drink than any other wine. It is beautifully clear and it intoxicates more speedily than any other wine, because it is very heating.

Let me tell you next of stones that burn like logs. It is a fact that throughout the province of Cathay there is a sort of black stone, which is dug out of veins in the hillsides and burns like logs. These stones keep a fire going better than wood. I assure you that, if you put them on the fire in the evening and see that they are well alight, they will continue to burn all night, so that you will find them still glowing in the morning. They do not give off flames, except a little when they are first kindled, just as charcoal does, and once they have caught fire they give out great heat. And you must know that these stones are burnt throughout the province of Cathay. It is true that they also have plenty of firewood. But the population is so enormous and there are so many bath-houses and baths continually being heated, that the wood could not possibly suffice, since there is no one who does not go to a bath-house at least three times a week and take a bath, and in winter every day, if he can manage it. And every man of rank or means has his own bathroom in his house, where he takes a bath. So it is clear that there could never be enough wood to maintain such a conflagration. So these stones, being very plentiful and very cheap, effect a great saving of wood.

To return to the provision of grain, you may take it for a fact that the Great Khan, when he sees that the harvests are plentiful and corn is cheap, accumulates vast quantities of it and stores it in huge granaries, where it is so carefully preserved that it remains unspoilt for three or four years. So he builds up a stock of every sort of grain – wheat, barley, millet, rice, panic, and others – in great abundance. Then, when it happens that some crops fail and there is a dearth of grain, he draws on these stocks. If the price is running at a bezant for a measure of wheat, for instance, he supplies four measures for the same sum. And he releases enough for all, so that everyone has plenty of corn to meet his needs. In this way he sees to it that none of his subjects need ever go short. And this he does throughout all parts of his empire.

Let me now tell you how the Great Khan bestows charity on the poor people of Khan-balik. When he learns that some family of honest and respectable people have been impoverished by some misfortune or disabled from working by illness, so that they have no means of earning their daily bread, he sees to it that such families (which may consist of six to ten persons or more) are given enough to cover their expenses for the whole year. These families, at the time appointed, go to the officials whose task it is to superintend the Great Khan's expenditure and who live in a palatial building assigned to their office. And each one produces a certificate of the sum paid to him for his subsistence the year before, and provision is made for them at the same rate this year. This provision includes clothing inasmuch as the Great Khan receives a tithe of all the wool, silk, and hemp used for cloth-making. He has these materials woven into cloth in a specially appointed building in which they are stored. Since all the crafts are under obligation to devote one day a week to working on his behalf, he has this cloth made up into garments, which he gives to the poor families in accordance with their needs for winter and for summer wear. He also provides clothing for his armies by having woollen cloth woven in every city as a contribution towards the payment of its tithe.

You must understand that the Tartars according to their ancient customs, before they became familiar with the doctrines of the idolaters, never used to give any alms. Indeed, when a poor man came to them, they would drive him off with maledictions, saying: 'Go with God's curse upon you! If he had loved you as he loves me, he would have blessed you with prosperity!' But since the sages of the idolaters, in particular the *Bakhshi* of whom I have spoken above, preached to the Great Khan that it was a good work to provide for the poor and that their idols would be greatly pleased by it, he was induced to make such provision as I have described. No one who cares to go to his court in quest of bread is ever turned away empty-handed. Everyone receives a portion. And not a day passes but twenty or thirty thousand bowls of rice, millet, and panic are doled out and given away by the officials appointed. And this goes on all the year round. For this amazing and stupendous munificence which the Great Khan exercises towards the poor, all the people hold him in such esteem that they revere him as a god.

There are also in the city of Khan-balik, including Christians, Saracens, and Cathayans, about 5,000 astrologers and soothsayers, for whom the Great Khan makes yearly provision of food and clothing as he does for the poor. These regularly practice their art in the city. They have a sort of almanack in which are written the movements of the planets through the constellations, hour by hour and minute by minute, throughout the year. Every year these astrologers, Christian, Saracen, and Cathayan, each sect on its own account, examine in this almanack the course and disposition of the whole year and of each particular moon. For they search out and discover what sort of conditions each moon of the year will produce in accordance with the natural course and disposition of the planets and constellations and their special influences: in such-and-such a month there will be thunderstorms, in another earthquakes, in another lightning and heavy rain, in yet another deadly outbreaks of pestilence and wars and civil dissensions. And so month by month in accordance with their findings. And they will declare that so it should happen in harmony with the natural and orderly sequence of things, but God may send more or less. So they will make many little booklets in which they will set down everything that is due to happen in the course of the year, moon by moon. These booklets are called *tacuim* and are sold at a groat apiece to anyone who cares to buy, so that he may know what will happen throughout the year. And those who prove to be the most accurate in their predictions will be reckoned the most accomplished masters of their art and will gain the greatest honour.

If anyone proposes to embark on some important enterprise or to travel somewhere on a trading venture or on other business, or has in mind some other project whose outcome he would like to know, he will consult the astrologers, telling them the year, month, hour, and minute of his nativity. This he is able to do, because in accordance with their custom everyone is taught from birth what he must say about his nativity, and parents are careful to note the particulars in a book. They divide the years into cycles of twelve, each with its own sign: the first bears the sign of the lion, the second of the ox, the third of the dragon, the fourth of the dog, and so on up to twelve. So, when a man is asked when he was born, he answers 'in a year of the lion, on such-and-such a day or night, hour, and minute of such-and-such a moon', according as the time and the year-sign may have been. When they have completed the cycle of twelve years, they begin again at the first sign and repeat the series, always in the same order. So, when anyone asks an astrologer or soothsayer how his proposed venture will turn out and tells him the hour and minute of his nativity and the sign of the year, then the soothsayer, having ascertained under which constellation and which planet he was born, will predict in due sequence all that is to happen to him on his travels and what fortune, good or bad, will attend his undertaking. Likewise, the inquirer may be warned, if he is a merchant, that the planet then in the ascendant will be hostile to his venture, so that he should await the ascendancy of one more favourable; or that the constellation directly facing the gate by which he is planning to leave the city will be adverse to the one under which he was born, so that he should leave by another gate or wait till the constellation has moved past; or that in such a place and on such a date he will encounter robbers, in another he will be assailed by rain and storm, in another his horse will break a leg, here his trafficking will involve him in loss, there it will bring in a profit. So the soothsayer will foretell the vicissitudes of his journey, propitious or disastrous, according to the sequence of favourable or unfavourable constellations.

As I have already said, the people of Cathay are all idolaters. Every man has in his house an image hanging on his chamber wall which represents the High God of Heaven, or at least a tablet on which the name of God is written. And every day they cense this with a thurible and worship it with uplifted hands, gnashing their teeth three times and praying that the god will give them a long and happy life, good health, and a sound understanding. From him they ask nothing else. But down below on the ground they have another image representing Natigai, the god of earthly things, who guides the course of all that is born on earth. They make him with a wife and children and worship him in the same way, with incense and gnashing of teeth and uplifted hands; and to him they pray for good weather and harvests and children and the like.

They surpass other nations in the excellence of their manners and their knowledge of many subjects, since they devote much time to their study and to the acquisition of knowledge. They speak in an agreeable and orderly manner, greet one another courteously with bright and cheerful faces, are dignified in their demeanour, cleanly at table, and so forth. But they have no regard for the welfare of their souls, caring only for the nurture of their bodies and for their own happiness. Concerning the soul, they believe indeed that it is immortal, but in this fashion. They hold that as soon as a man is dead he enters into another body; and according as he has conducted himself well or ill in life, he passes from good to better or from bad to worse. That is to say, if he is a man of humble rank and has behaved well and virtuously in life, he will be reborn after death from a gentlewoman and will be a gentleman, and thereafter from the womb of a noblewoman and will become a nobleman; and so he follows an ever upward path culminating in assumption into the Deity. But, if he is a man of good birth and has behaved badly, he will be reborn as the son of a peasant; from a peasant's life he will pass to a dog's and so continually downwards.

They treat their father and mother with profound respect. If it should happen that a child does anything to displease his parents or fails to remember them in their need, there is a department of state whose sole function it is to impose severe penalties on those who are found guilty of such ingratitude.

Perpetrators of various crimes who are caught and put in prison, if they have not been set free at the time appointed by the Great Khan for the release of prisoners, which recurs every three years, are then let out; but they are branded on the jaw, so that they may be recognized.

The present Khan prohibited all the gambling and cheating that used to be more prevalent among them than anywhere else in the world. To cure them of the habit he would say: 'I have acquired you by force of arms and all that you possess is mine. So, if you gamble, you are gambling with my property.' He did not, however, make this a pretext to take anything from them.

*

I will not omit to tell you about the behaviour of the Khan's people and noblemen when they come into his presence. First, all those who are within half a mile from the Great Khan, wherever he may be, show their reverence for his majesty by conducting themselves deferentially, peaceably, and quietly so that no hub-bub or uproar may be heard, nor the voice of anyone shouting or talking loudly. Next, every baron or nobleman continually carries with him a little vessel of pleasing design into which he spits so long as he is in the hall, so that no one may make so bold as to spit on the floor; and when he has spat he covers it up and keeps it. Likewise they have handsome slippers of white leather, which they carry about with them. When they have come to court, if they are about to enter the hall at the Lord's invitation, they put on these white slippers and hand their others to the attendants, so as not to dirty the beautiful and elaborate carpets of silk, wrought in gold and other colours.

From Peking to Bengal

Let us now leave the city of Khan-balik and travel into Cathay, so that you may learn something of its grandeurs and its treasures.

You must understand that Messer Marco himself was sent by the Great Khan as an emissary towards the west, on a journey of fully four months from Khan-balik. So we will tell you what he saw on the way, going and coming.

[. . .]

On leaving Ch'êng-tu-fu the traveller rides for five days through plain and valley, passing villages and hamlets in plenty. The people here live on the yield of the earth. The country is infested with lions, bears, and other wild beasts. There is some local industry, in the weaving of fine sendal and other fabrics. This country is part of Ch'êng-tu-fu province. But at the end of the five days the route enters another province whose name is Tibet.*

The province of Tibet is terribly devastated, for it was ravaged in a campaign by Mongu Khan. There are many

---

* Polo's account of 'Tebet' applies primarily to districts now included in the provinces of Sze-ch'wan and Yün-nan to the east of the present Tibetan frontier.

towns and villages and hamlets lying ruined and desolate.

This country produces canes of immense size and girth; indeed I can assure you that they grow to about three palms in circumference and a good fifteen paces in length, the distance from one knot to the next amounting to fully three palms. Merchants and other travellers who are passing through this country at night use these canes as fuel because, when they are alight, they make such a popping and banging that lions and bears and other beasts of prey are scared away in terror and dare not on any account come near the fire. So fires of this sort are made by travellers to protect their own animals from the savage predators with which the country is infested. Let me tell you – for it is well worth telling – how it happens that the crackling of these canes is so loud and terrifying and what effect it produces. You must understand that the canes are taken when quite green and thrown on a fire made of a substantial pile of logs. When they have lain for some time on a fire of this size, they begin to warp and to burst, and then they make such a bang that it can be heard at nights fully ten miles away. Anyone who is not accustomed to the noise is startled out of his wits by it; it is such a terrifying sound to hear. I assure you that horses that have never heard it before are so scared when they hear it that they snap their halters and all the cords that tether them and take to their heels. Many travellers have experienced this. So, when they have horses that are known never to have heard this noise, they bandage their eyes and shackle all the feet with iron fetlocks. Then, when they hear the crackling of the canes, however hard they try to bolt, they cannot do it. And by this means travellers keep safe at nights; both they and their beasts, from the lions and ounces and other dangerous beasts that abound in these parts.

This desolate country, infested by dangerous wild beasts, extends for twenty days' journey, without shelter or food except perhaps every third or fourth day, when the traveller may find some habitation where he can renew his stock of provisions. Then he reaches a region with villages and hamlets in plenty and a few towns perched on precipitous crags. Here there prevails a marriage custom of which I will tell you. It is such that no man would ever on any account take a virgin to wife. For they say that a woman is worthless unless she has had knowledge of many men. They argue that she must have displeased the gods, because if she enjoyed the favour of their idols then men would desire her and consort with her. So they deal with their womenfolk in this way. When it happens that men from a foreign land are passing through this country and have pitched their tents and made a camp, the matrons from neighbouring villages and hamlets bring their daughters to these camps, to the number of twenty or forty, and beg the travellers to take them and lie with them. So these choose the girls who please them best, and the others return home disconsolate. So long as they remain, the visitors are free to take their pleasure with the women and use them as they will, but they are not allowed to carry them off anywhere else. When the men have worked their will and are ready to be gone, then it is the custom for every man to give to the woman with whom he has lain some trinket or token so that she can show, when she comes to marry, that she has had a lover. In this way custom requires every girl to wear more than a score of such tokens hung round her neck to show that she has had lovers in plenty and plenty of men have lain with her. And she who has most tokens and can show that she has had most lovers and that most men have lain with her is the most highly esteemed and the most acceptable as a wife; for they say that she is the most favoured by the gods. And when they have taken a wife in this way they prize her highly; and they account it a grave offence for any man to touch another's wife, and they all strictly abstain from such an act. So much, then, for this marriage custom, which fully merits a description. Obviously the country is a fine one to visit for a lad from sixteen to twenty-four.

The natives are idolaters and out-and-out bad. They deem it no sin to rob and maltreat and are the greatest rogues and the greatest robbers in the world. They live by the chase and by their herds and the fruits of the earth. The country abounds with animals that produce musk, which in their language are called *gudderi*. They are so plentiful that you can smell musk everywhere. I have already explained that a sac in the form of a tumour and filled with blood grows next to the beast's navel, and this blood is musk. But I must add that once in every moon the sac becomes overcharged with blood and discharges its contents. So it happens, since these animals are very plentiful here, that they discharge their musk in many places, so that the whole country is pervaded with the scent. The rascally natives have many excellent dogs, who catch great numbers of these animals; so they have no lack of musk.

The natives have no coinage and do not use the Khan's paper currency; but for money they use salt. They are very poorly clad, in skins, canvas, and buckram. They speak a language of their own and call themselves 'Tibet'.

This province of Tibet is of immense size and lies on the confines of Manzi and many other provinces. The natives are idolaters and notorious brigands. The province is so huge that it contains eight kingdoms and a great many cities and towns. In many places there are rivers and lakes and mountains, in which gold-dust is found in great quantity. There is also great abundance of cinnamon. In this province coral fetches a high price, for it is hung round the necks of women and of idols with great joy. The province produces plenty of camlets and other cloths of gold, silk, and fustian, and many sorts of spice that were never seen in our country. Here are to be found the most skilful enchanters and the best astrologers according to their usage that exist in any of the regions hereabouts. Among other wonders they bring on tempests and thunder-storms when they wish and stop them at any time. They perform the most potent enchantments and the greatest marvels to hear and to behold by diabolic arts, which it is better not to relate in our book, or men might marvel over-much. Their customs are disagreeable. They have mastiffs as big as donkeys, very good at pulling down game, including wild cattle, which are plentiful there and of great size and ferocity. They also have a great variety of other hunting dogs, besides excellent lanner and saker falcons, good fliers and apt for hawking. Before leaving Tibet, of which we have now given a full account, let me make it clear that it belongs to the Great Khan, as do all the other kingdoms and provinces and regions described in this book, except only the provinces mentioned at the beginning of our book which belong to the son of Arghun, as I have told you. So you may understand from this, without further indication, that with this exception the provinces described in this book are all subject to the Great Khan.

We will tell you next of the province of Kaindu, which lies towards the west. It has only one king. The people are idolaters and subject to the Great Khan. It has cities and towns in plenty. The chief city, also called Kaindu, lies near the entrance to the province. There is also a lake in which are found many pearls – pure white but not round, being rather knobbly as though four, five, six, or more were joined together. The Great Khan will not let anyone take them; for if all the pearls that were found there were taken out, so many would be taken that they would be cheap and lose their value. So the Great Khan, when he has a mind, has pearls taken from it for his own use only; but no one else may take them on pain of death. There is also a mountain there in which is found a sort of stone called turquoise. These are very fine gems and very plentiful. But the Great Khan does not allow them to be taken except at his bidding.

Let me tell you that in this province there prevails a usage concerning women such as I will describe to you. A man does not think it an outrage if a stranger or some other man makes free with his wife or daughter or sister or any woman he may have in his house. But it is taken as a favour when anyone lies with them. For they say that by this act their gods and idols are propitiated, so as to enrich them with temporal blessings in great abundance. And for that reason they deal with their wives in the following open-handed fashion. You must know that when a man of this country sees that a stranger is coming to his house to lodge, or that he is entering his house without intending to lodge, he immediately walks out, telling his wife to let the stranger have his will without reservation. Then he goes his way to his fields or vineyards and does not return so long as the stranger remains in his house. And I assure you that he often stays three days and lies in bed with this wittol's wife. And as a sign that he is in the house he hangs out his cap or some other token. This is an indication that he is within. And the wretched wittol, so long as he sees this sign in his house, does not return. This usage prevails throughout the province. The Great Khan has forbidden it; but they continue to observe it nonetheless, since, as they are all addicted to it, there is no one to accuse another. There are some residents in the villages and homesteads perched on crags by the wayside who have beautiful wives and offer them freely to passing traders. And the traders give the women a piece of some fine cloth, perhaps a yard or so, or some other trinket of trifling value. Having taken his pleasure for a while, the trader mounts his horse and rides away. Then the husband and wife call after him in mockery: 'Hi, you there – you that are riding off! Show us what you are taking with you that is ours! Let us see, ne'er-do-well, what profit you have made! Look at what you have left to us – what you have thrown away and forgotten.' And he flourishes the cloth they have gained from him. 'We have got this of yours, you poor fool, and you have nothing to show for it!' So they mock at him. And so they continue to act.

Let me tell you next about their money. They have gold in bars and weigh it out by *saggi*; and it is valued according to its weight. But they have no coined money bearing a stamp. For small change they do as follows. They have salt water from which they make salt by boiling it in pans. When they have boiled it for an hour, they let it solidify in moulds, forming blocks of the size of a twopenny loaf, flat below and rounded on top. When the blocks are ready, they are laid on heated-stones beside the fire to dry and harden. On these blocks they set the Great Khan's stamp. And currency of this sort is made only by his agents. Eighty of these blocks are worth a *saggio* of gold. But traders come with these blocks to the people who live among the mountains in wild and out-of-the-way places and receive a *saggio* of gold for sixty, fifty, or forty blocks, according as the place is more isolated and cut off from cities and civilized people. Here the natives cannot dispose of their gold and other wares, such as musk, for want of purchasers. So they sell their gold cheap, because they find it in rivers and lakes as you have heard. These traders travel all over the highlands of Tibet, where the salt money is also current. They make an immense profit, because these people use this salt in food as well as for buying the necessities of life; but in the cities they almost invariably use fragments of the blocks for food and spend the unbroken blocks.

There are vast numbers here of the beasts that produce musk, and hunters catch them and take great quantities of the musk. There are plenty of good fish, which are caught in the same lake that produces the pearls. There are also lions, lynxes, bears, stags, and roebuck in plenty, and birds of every sort abound. There is no grape wine, but wine is made of wheat and rice with many spices, and a very good drink it is. The province is also a great source of cloves, which grow on a little tree with leaves like laurel but slightly longer and narrower, and little white flowers like clove-pinks. There is also ginger in abundance and cinnamon, not to speak of spices that never come to our country.

When the traveller leaves the city of Kaindu, he rides for ten days through a country not lacking in towns and villages, and well stocked with game, both bird and beast. The people have the same manners and customs as those I have described. At the end of these ten days he reaches a great river called Brius, which is the farther boundary of the province of Kaindu. In it are found great quantities of gold dust. The district is also rich in cinnamon. This river runs into the Ocean.

On the farther side of the river Brius lies Kara-jang, a province of such size that it contains no less than seven kingdoms. It lies towards the west, and the inhabitants are idolaters and subject to the Great Khan. Its king is his son, whose name is Essen-Temur, a very great king and rich and powerful. He rules his land well and justly; for he is a wise and upright man.

After leaving the river, the traveller continues westwards for five days, through a country with numerous cities and towns which breeds excellent horses. The people live by rearing animals and tilling the soil. They speak a language of their own, which is very difficult to understand. At the end of the five days he reaches the capital of the kingdom, which is called Yachi, a large and splendid city. Here there are traders and craftsmen in plenty. The inhabitants are of several sorts: there are some who worship Mahomet, some idolaters, and a few Nestorian Christians. Both wheat and rice are plentiful; but wheat bread is not eaten because in this province it is unwholesome. The natives eat rice, and also make it into a drink with spices, which is very fine and clear and makes a man drunk like wine. For money they use white cowries, i.e. the sea-shells that are used to make necklaces for dogs: 80 cowries are equivalent to 1 *saggio* of silver, which is worth 2 Venetian groats, and 8 *saggi* of fine silver may be taken to equal 1 of fine gold. They also have brine wells, from which they make salt that is used for food by all the inhabitants of the country. And I assure you that the king derives great profit from this salt. The men here do not mind if one touches another's wife, so long as it is with her consent.

Before leaving this kingdom let me tell you something which I had forgotten. There is a lake here, some 100 miles in circumference, in which there is a vast quantity of fish, the best in the world. They are of great size and of all kinds. The natives eat flesh raw – poultry, mutton, beef, and buffalo meat. The poorer sort go to the shambles and take the raw liver as soon as it is drawn from the beasts; then they chop it small, put it in garlic sauce and eat it there and then. And they do likewise with every other kind of flesh. The gentry also eat their meat raw; but they have it minced very small, put it in garlic sauce flavoured with spices and then eat it as readily as we eat cooked meat.

On leaving Yachi and continuing westwards for ten days, the traveller reaches the kingdom of Kara-jang, the capital of which is also called Kara-jang. The people are idolaters and subject to the Great Khan. The king is Hukaji, a son of the Great Khan. In this province gold dust is found in the rivers, and gold in bigger nuggets in the lakes and mountains. They have so much of it that they give a *saggio* of gold for six of silver. Here too the cowries of which I have spoken are used for money. They are not found in this province, but come here from India.

In this province live huge snakes and serpents* of such a size that no one could help being amazed even to hear of them. They are loathsome creatures to behold. Let me tell you just how big they are. You may take it for a fact that there are some of them ten paces in length that are as thick as a stout cask: for their girth runs to about ten palms. These are the biggest. They have two squat legs in front near the head, which have no feet but simply three claws, two small and one bigger, like the claws of a falcon or a lion. They have enormous heads and eyes

---

* Evidently crocodiles.

so bulging that they are bigger than loaves. Their mouth is big enough to swallow a man at one gulp. Their teeth are huge. All in all, the monsters are of such inordinate bulk and ferocity that there is neither man nor beast but goes in fear of them. There are also smaller ones, not exceeding eight paces in length, or six or it may be five.

Let me tell you now how these monsters are trapped. You must know that by day they remain underground because of the great heat; at nightfall, they sally out to hunt and feed and seize whatever prey they can come by. They go down to drink at streams and lakes and springs. They are so bulky and heavy and of such a girth that when they pass through sand on their nightly search for food or drink they scoop out a furrow through the sand that looks as if a butt full of wine had been rolled that way. Now the hunters who set out to catch them lay traps at various places in the trails that show which way the snakes are accustomed to go down the banks into the water. These are made by embedding in the earth a stout wooden stake to which is fixed a sharp steel tip like a razor-blade or lance-head, projecting about a palm's breadth beyond the stake and slanting in the direction from which the serpents approach. This is covered with sand, so that nothing of the stake is visible. Traps of this sort are laid in great numbers. When the snake, or rather the serpent, comes down the trail to drink, he runs full-tilt into the steel, so that it pierces his chest and rips his belly right to the navel and he dies on the spot. The hunter knows that the serpent is dead by the cry of the birds, and then he ventures to approach his prey. Otherwise he dare not draw near.

When hunters have trapped a serpent by this means, they draw out the gall from the belly and sell it for a high price, for you must know that it makes a potent medicine. If a man is bitten by a mad dog, he is given a drop of it to drink – the weight of a halfpenny – and he is cured forthwith. And when a woman is in labour and cries aloud with the pangs of travail, she is given a drop of the serpent's gall and as soon as she has drunk it she is delivered of her child forthwith. Its third use is when someone is afflicted by any sort of growth: he puts a drop of this gall on it and is cured in a day or two. For these reasons the gall of this serpent is highly prized in these provinces. The flesh also commands a good price, because it is very good to eat and is esteemed as a delicacy.

Another thing about these serpents: they go to the dens where lions and bears and other beasts of prey have their cubs and gobble them up – parents as well as young – if they can get at them.

Let me tell you further that this province produces a sturdy breed of horses, which are exported when young for sale in India. And you must know that it is the custom to remove two or three joints of the tail-bone, so that the horse cannot flick the rider with its tail or swish it when galloping; for it is reckoned unsightly for a horse to gallop with swishing tail. The horsemen here ride with long stirrups after the French fashion – long, that is, in contrast to the short stirrups favoured by the Tartars and most other races who go in for archery, since they use their stirrups for standing upright when they shoot.

For armour they wear cuirasses of buffalo hide. They

carry lances and shields. They also use cross-bows, with all the quarrels dipped in poison. All the natives, women as well as men, especially those who are bent on evil courses, carry poison about with them. If it should chance that anyone is caught after committing a crime for which he is liable to suffer torture, rather than face the penalty of the scourge, he puts the poison in his mouth and swallows it, so as to die as quickly as possible. But, since the authorities are well aware of this trick, they always have some dog's dung handy, so that if a prisoner swallows poison for this purpose he is immediately made to swallow the dung and so vomit up the poison. Such is the remedy they have found for this practice, and it is a well-tried one. Another practice of theirs, before they were conquered by the Great Khan, was this. If it happened that a gentleman of quality, with a fine figure, or a 'good shadow', came to lodge in the house of a native of this province, they would murder him in the night, by poison or other means, so that he died. You must not suppose that they did this in order to rob him; they did it rather because they believed that his 'good shadow' and the good grace with which he was blessed and his intelligence and soul would remain in the house. In this way many met their deaths before the conquest. Since then – that is, during the last thirty-five years or so – they have abandoned this evil practice for fear of the Great Khan, who has strictly forbidden it.